SPINNER'S WICKET

SPINNER'S WICKET

Ray Illingworth

AS TOLD TO PETER SMITH

STANLEY PAUL/LONDON

STANLEY PAUL & CO LTD
178–202 Great Portland Street, London W1

AN IMPRINT OF THE HUTCHINSON GROUP

London Melbourne Sydney
Auckland Bombay Toronto
Johannesburg New York

First published 1969

*This book has been set in Baskerville, printed in Great Britain
on Antique Wove paper by The Camelot Press Ltd., London and Southampton,
and bound by Wm. Brendon, Tiptree, Essex*

CONTENTS

ILLUSTRATIONS

I

Growing up

Some are born with silver spoons in their mouths. I was born in Pudsey. You can't be luckier than that if you want to play cricket.

John Tunnicliffe, Major Booth, Herbert Sutcliffe and his son, Billy, Sir Len Hutton and Harry Halliday all came from this village which lies between the cities of Bradford and Leeds.

So it was natural that I should want to follow them into the county side.

I arrived in the world on June 8, 1932. My father was a cabinet-maker, but when I was only five we moved to the neighbouring village of Farsley where his business premises were situated.

I attended Frances Street School, Farsley, and later went on to the Wesley Street School.

Dad used to play cricket locally, and in the school holidays he often used to slip along to the park and join us in our impromptu 'Test' matches.

He made me my first bat, too. It was not one of those beautifully turned modern pieces, but it was still my most prized possession at the time. I kept it until he managed to purchase a brand new one for me. That was something of an achievement in itself, because all forms of sports equipment were hard to come by during the war years when I was growing up.

In those uneasy times the parks and open spaces didn't often get cut because there was little petrol to be spared for mowing. But that didn't stop the local lads in our district from preparing their own pitch.

We called it the Wreck! We dug it up, bought seed and

relaid it and kept it in trim with one hand-mower and a pair of shears. One night disaster struck. A herd of cows strayed on to our precious wicket. The farmer drove them off, but not before they had churned up the whole area.

We had to spend most of our pocket money on getting the pitch level again, but then we would go to almost any sacrifice to stage our games.

At school, like any other cricket-mad kid, I wanted to be in action all the time. I opened the batting and bowled seamers. In fact, it was only by chance that I thought of turning to off-spin.

We were playing Wyther Park School from Leeds in a challenge match and I was bowling my seamers. Suddenly I sent down a slower one which turned quite a bit and the master who was umpiring for Wyther Park, said to me: 'If you can bowl off-breaks like that, lad, don't waste your time on seamers.' That was the first occasion anyone had suggested I should change my bowling.

I became captain of the school eleven and we were unbeaten when schools cricket returned at the end of the war. I think I averaged a hundred with the bat and my wickets cost around two a piece.

We were coached by Sam Blackburn, one of many who devoted themselves to teaching youngsters in that part of Yorkshire. Indeed, I think this is one of the reasons why Yorkshire has always produced so much cricketing talent. Such a lot of people have been willing to give up their spare time to coach and instruct the lads and I, for one, am very grateful for all the assistance they gave me in my formative years.

Wesley Street did not have their own playing field during the war as they have today, but Farsley Cricket Club were very good in allowing the school to use their ground for matches. That is how I came to get an invitation to play for the second eleven. Their officials would come along to the school matches and it was the natural sequence of events that youngsters who showed promise would progress into the village teams.

I was about fourteen when I first played for Farsley's second eleven and my great cricketing idol was Len Hutton. Who else for a lad from Pudsey?

I used to watch him in those wartime league matches. Grandfather would say to me: 'I think you would put your very last halfpenny in his collection'—and I would have done.

I even played truant from school to watch him. That was when the Indian touring team were playing Yorkshire at Bradford Park in 1946.

Three of us took the day off. We set off so early that we were at the front of the queue outside the ground when a photographer climbed on the perimeter wall and took a picture of the waiting crowds, with us well to the fore. Unfortunately for us, the picture appeared in the *Yorkshire Evening Post* that night. The Head saw it. Talk about your sins finding you out!

The Head was a good sport. He gave us a thorough ticking off, with the customary warning that we must never do anything like that again, but I think he had a sneaking regard for our nerve. After all, it was Len Hutton we had gone to watch!

Len was an inspiration for any starry-eyed cricket lad. To see him play on a turning wicket was an education in itself. The ball never seemed to turn when he was batting. He was always in such a sound position to play his strokes. He possessed that uncanny knack of being able to use his bat to cushion the effect of spin. The bat would just relax and the ball would drop stone dead at his feet. I have certainly never seen any other batsman do this with such technical perfection.

When I left school I went straight into my father's furniture and cabinet-making business. I was always fairly useful at making things and I liked the work. I never fancied myself at an office desk or anything of that nature.

I was lucky, too, because father was always willing to give me time off to play cricket, and soon I won my place in Farsley's first team, batting around six or seven and bowling first change.

The Bradford League, in which Farsley competed, contained a number of experienced professionals, among them the West Indies Test player, Martindale, Bill Copson, the Derbyshire and England fast bowler, and Yorkshire stars like Arthur Booth and Horace Fisher.

I found it really hard work because at sixteen I was still rather small in build—I grew a lot between seventeen and eighteen—and I didn't seem to have the power to get the ball away when I was batting. I remember playing for Farsley's junior side which won the Bradford League title, and Brian Close was in one of the rival teams. I thought then how much bigger and stronger he was than I—he looked a man already, although he was only a year older.

I have already mentioned how I always wanted to be involved in the game. That's how I came to try my hand as a wicket-keeper in Sunday matches, at least until Donald Waterhouse, a fine League player, advised me to pack it up. 'You'll be breaking your fingers, lad. Stick to your batting and bowling.' So I did.

I also received considerable help from George Hutton and Norman Jackson who were responsible for coaching youngsters at the Pudsey St Lawrence Club. George was a very good batsman in the Bradford League and Norman opened the bowling for Pudsey St Lawrence and was also a good striker of the ball. We used to go twice a week for evening instruction.

Despite my moment as an off-spinner in that school match, I continued to bowl at medium pace. Then, one afternoon, I was taking part in a Bradford League fixture at Saltaire. We were bowled out for 58 on a wet track and they were 30 for one when Jackie Firth, the Yorkshire and Leicestershire wicket-keeper, who was the professional at Farsley, tossed the ball to me and said: 'Why don't you bowl some spinners?'

He had seen me experimenting with them in the nets. I gave it a go and took five for 5, and won us the match!

I have written about my keenness for cricket, but I should add that as a lad I was probably just as proficient at soccer. I played in the local league as a wing-half. Football League scouts were often turning up at these matches and Aston Villa, Huddersfield and Bradford City invited me for trials.

I talked it over with Norman Jackson who not only helped with the coaching for the Pudsey St. Lawrence club but was on the committee of the local football club. He advised me to go home and think over the implications of going for a dual sporting career.

Father was very much against my playing soccer because he was afraid I might break a leg and ruin my opportunities as a cricketer. At that time there was not the big money incentives in soccer to lure a youngster into League football. After some heart-searching I turned down the trials.

I know that such people as Denis Compton, Willie Watson and Arthur Milton, to name just a few, have succeeded in reaching the top at both games. But nowadays with soccer encroaching even more into the cricket season, I think it is becoming more difficult to reach international status at both. The danger must be that you will fall between the two stools and fail to rise above average standard at either game.

This situation may suit some players, but I have always believed in disciplining all my time and energies to becoming a leading player at one sport. All my other recreational pursuits such as golf, are subordinate to my cricket.

The Yorkshire County Cricket Club, with their splendidly organized system of coaching, first invited me to their nets when I was sixteen. Arthur Mitchell, Bill Bowes and later

Maurice Leyland, were in charge and any lad who went to the nets was lucky, indeed, to have their cumulative experience at his disposal.

They must have thought something of me because I kept going back and was eventually picked for the Yorkshire Federation, a team of under eighteens chosen from the various leagues.

The county club do not actually select the team, but they have a say in its composition.

In 1948 we went down to Sussex and I found myself in the same side as Brian Close and Freddie Trueman. Incidentally, the first time I saw Fred I thought he was a left-arm spin bowler! We went out on the ground for a loosener-up before the start and Fred started wheeling them down left-arm—and looking quite impressive too. I was amazed when the captain gave him the ball to open the bowling and he came rushing up off 20 yards, bowling fast right-arm! I never actually saw Freddie bowl his left-arm trundlers in a match but, knowing him, I bet he could if he set his mind to it.

In October, 1950, I was called up for my National Service in the Royal Air Force. I had been granted a month's deferment in order that I could finish the season playing for Yorkshire Seconds, and I was posted to Cheltenham for my square-bashing.

By a stroke of good fortune, I met an officer who came from Dishforth, which is only about 30 miles or so from my home. He was a keen cricketer and he recommended me for a posting to the R.A.F. station there. I worked mostly in the P.T.I. sports store and found plenty of opportunities for playing cricket.

The R.A.F. team included a number of talented young players, among them Freddie Trueman, Freddie Titmus, Jim Parks, Roly Thomson and Bob Hurst. We made 500 in a day against Worcestershire when Jim Parks and I put on 100 in 34 minutes.

2

Debut for Yorkshire

Late in the summer of 1951 I was due to turn out for
Combined Services against Warwickshire, the eventual
county champions that season, at Edgbaston, when I was
told to report to Headingley. Yorkshire had called me up to
make my first-team debut against Hampshire, and the
Air Force authorities sportingly agreed to my release.

Everything looked set for a huge Yorkshire score when
Norman Yardley, returning from his duties as chairman of
the England Test Selectors, won the toss on a lovely August
morning, and I settled down to enjoy a feast of run-making.

Len Hutton wasn't playing and the innings was opened
by Harry Halliday and Ted Lester. Unhappily for them—
and Yorkshire—Vic Cannings, the Hampshire seam bowler,
was in deadly form with the new ball.

He kept bringing it back sharply and in ten electrifying
overs (they certainly gave a series of shocks to this new boy!)
Cannings bowled Halliday, Lester, Vic Wilson and Billy
Sutcliffe at a personal cost of 22. We were 40 for four and
Raymond Illingworth was walking out to join his skipper,
Norman Yardley.

I tried to look as calm as possible, but I could feel some
definite thumpings around the rib cage as I surveyed the
Hampshire fielders. They were clustered in hungry looking
groups just waiting to pocket me—that was, unless Cannings
himself didn't knock over my castle!

Amid all this forbidding atmosphere, I found one very
large lump of good fortune in the shape of Norman. He was a
constant source of encouragement as I struggled to survive
those early overs.

At that time I liked to use the cover drive and Norman told me not to be afraid to play the stroke. Well, things worked out all right for me because I managed to help Norman put on more than 100 and my own contribution was 56.

A newspaper clipping of that match recorded:

'Illingworth played an invaluable part by staying with Yardley for two hours and making his debut for the county with a stylish 56 which included seven fours. At times his stroke play was delightful and some of his cover drives were superb and in the best Hutton traditions.'

The notice was probably unduly kind to a raw nineteen-year-old colt. All the same it was a great personal thrill to see my name even associated with such a mighty man.

I cannot actually recall the first time I spoke to Len, but I do have a recollection of joining him at a net session.

Understandably, I was anxious to show up well in front of my hero when he bowled at me. Instead I had some difficulty in timing my strokes and Arthur Mitchell had to come into the net and explain how I was playing the wrong line.

The county players didn't use any kid-glove methods when the colts practised with them. They had undergone tough apprenticeships themselves and it had done them no harm. So they saw no reason to treat us softly.

At one session Alec Coxon, who played for England against the Australians in 1948, bowled me neck and crop with three consecutive balls, but by that time in my cricket education, I think Arthur Mitchell reckoned I might make the grade.

Anyway, he shouted to me from the back of the net:

'What the bloody hell are you doing, letting them knock over your castle like that!'

His words had the desired effect. I got my head down and let the stumps have some peace!

When I completed my National Service with the Royal

Air Force, I returned to continue learning the furniture trade with my father but, of course, I was thinking whether I would be good enough to make a career as a professional cricketer.

I had a very good season in the Bradford League and finished only 90 short of 1,000 runs. I might have made it but I missed four games, because of service duties. I am told only two players, Hamer and Paynter, have achieved a thousand in the Bradford League.

I began playing regularly for Yorkshire in 1953. The batting line-up was formidable enough, with Len Hutton, Frank Lowson, Harry Halliday, Willie Watson and Norman Yardley, but the bowling was thin. Bob Appleyard was ill and Brian Close injured. Johnny Wardle and I were the spinners.

I made the best possible start to that season any youngster could have wished by scoring my first hundred for Yorkshire against Essex at Hull, after we had lost five wickets for 100-odd runs.

In describing my knock, Jim Kilburn in the *Yorkshire Post* wrote:

'Illingworth owed rather more to his lucky stars at the beginning of his innings. He was not missed, but there were half a dozen occasions when he was as nearly bowled as ever he will be without the bails falling. His early stroke play towards the faster bowling was inclined to be over casual, but once he had found the pace of the wicket he began to play beautiful cricket. His off-driving was firm and eager and he swung cheerfully at anything outside the leg stump, and when he reached 100 he had hit 10 boundaries, most of which would have been boundaries on a field twice the size —and there is no more extensive playing area in Yorkshire than this one at Anlaby Road.

'From 251 for 7 at the departure of Wardle from a mis-hit to mid-off, Yorkshire moved quietly on, with Brennan as an encouraginging partner to the triumphant Illingworth, whose century was completed at ten minutes past six after momentary and understandable fluttering in the nineties.

'Thereafter, Illingworth was in that batsman's heaven of accomplishment assured, all bowling seen and conquered, and day's end approaching in a heart's content of hitting. There is no century like the first one, made when it was wanted.

'Perhaps Essex might have been attacked even more vigorously in the final half-hour, for those minutes were borrowed from Monday, but when an eighth wicket offers a century stand, there is small scope for cavilling, and Illingworth could justifiably plead that four and a quarter hours at the wicket is a tiring experience.'

'White Rose', writing in the *Yorkshire Observer*, had this to say:

'For the third time on successive days the team's leading batsmen had fallen all too readily, and the position that Illingworth had to face was that Halliday, Hutton, Lester, Wilson and Watson all had been swept aside for a mere 104 in a surprising ascendancy by the Essex attack, with former England amateur, Trevor Bailey, as the spearhead.

'Most Colts would have been unnerved in such a situation but Illingworth's supreme confidence, discernment, punishing power and off-side stroke play particularly, made it an innings to remember.'

And Bill Bowes, in congratulating me, had this to say:

'His first century has been a long time coming, but the quality of his innings, when he had overcome his hesitant beginnings, was first class.

'His defence was certain. He played shots with equal sureness to all parts of the field and his driving was excellent to watch. Rarely did he lift the ball from the turf and behind his shots there was remarkable power. . . . I said it had been a big score a long time coming. I can remember five seasons ago at the Headingley nets. Johnny Wardle was bowling to Illingworth as a fifteen-year-old. Said Johnny: "I don't know who this youngster is but he will play for Yorkshire." '

Then Bill, a kindly person with a gift for imparting cricketing skills to young players, added this rider:

'Of course, Illingworth still has a good distance to travel. In Yorkshire we are not content with good county batsmen. They must earn consideration for England before we are impressed. . . .'

In the first month of that season I was top of the county averages, around the 60 mark, but I was getting my chances at No. Seven because at that time Vic Wilson and Ted Lester were struggling to find their form.

When the good wickets came in June and July, Len Hutton and Frank Lowson made a lot of runs and I must have gone some weeks without even batting. Still, I managed to end the season with 900 or so runs and about 90 wickets, which made me feel that I was on the way to proving myself in the first-class game.

Yet I had to wait until 1957 before I finally achieved a double of 1,000 runs and 100 wickets.

Although I did well enough in 1953, I soon discovered that I still had to convince some people that I was worth a regular place in the county team.

The following year the county had thirteen capped players and although I stayed with the team every match, I was often twelfth man, and one or two other counties began to show an interest in me.

Warwickshire asked permission to interview me and they offered me excellent terms, far better than I was receiving from Yorkshire. As an uncapped player I had to rely on match money, whereas Warwickshire were prepared to pay me £850 plus expenses. That was as much as the Yorkshire capped players were earning!

Match money worked out at around £8 or £9 for a home

match, £15 or £16 for an away game and out of that I had
to pay all my travelling expenses *and* for evening meals.
Frankly, I couldn't have managed at that time without the
help I received from my parents, who did so much, in so
many ways, to further my ambitions as a cricketer.

Warwickshire impressed me as a thoroughly efficient and
businesslike cricketing organization.

Their chairman travelled up to interview me and said:
'We would like you to come and play for us. We think that
if you do, you will become an England player.'

Now the Yorkshire attitude—at least that of the committee
—has always been that you play better under pressure. They
would always be letting you know, in one form or another,
that if you didn't do your stuff, there was someone else ready
to take over.

This approach can work out for some players. Others need
encouragement. They need to be told that they are good
players who could become England players.

I think this pressure from the top, this constant awareness
that you mustn't fail, is something which no other county
employs with quite the same emphasis. I know the competition for places is there, but in Yorkshire, where players have
no contracts, the risk of failure assumes far more importance
in the mind. Maybe Yorkshire can afford to ignore those who
consider, as I do, that this pressure on their players is wrong.
After all, they can point to their many Championship
triumphs as a justification for their methods, but a lot of disillusioned youngsters have joined other counties because
they didn't get the encouragement they needed. If the
pressures had been taken off of many of them, I am sure they
would have made their names in their native heath instead of
as exiles.

3

An ultimatum—and my cap

The offer from Warwickshire and the knowledge that one or two other counties would be ready to discuss terms, persuaded me to do something positive about my future.

I went to Norman Yardley in 1955 and asked him to inform the committee that if they didn't consider I was worth my cap, then they shouldn't expect to retain me any longer. I got my cap the next match.

Although the award of that cap seemed a long time arriving, I realized that I was far more fortunate than some other Yorkshire players.

Take the case of Doug Padgett. He made his county debut in 1951, the same year as I did, but it was 1958 before he finally received full county recognition.

Doug is the sort of player who gives his team 100 per cent effort all the time. You don't have to drive him, but he does need encouragement from time to time.

The best season he had was under Ronnie Burnet in 1959, because Ronnie went out of his way to tell him he was a good player. He gave Doug the self-confidence to play his strokes, and that simple psychology—call it what you will—did the trick. Doug scored more than 2,000 runs that summer.

Equally, certain players need pushing a little bit. I consider Ken Taylor to fall into this category. He had such a tremendous amount of natural ability, as a cricketer and footballer, that he never had to work really hard at his games. Yet in certain technical respects of his batting he might have profited by some direction, some instruction. He probably wouldn't have liked it because as a natural games player he would have found it irksome, but it might have made him an even better performer. Now he has emigrated to South Africa.

People sitting around the boundary watching the county game may not always appreciate the mental pressures experienced by those playing out in the middle.

I believe that after such a long period in the game I have learned to live with the stresses and strains which six-days-a-week cricket produces, but back in my early days with Yorkshire life wasn't as easy.

I have very vivid memories of dropping a catch on the boundary off Bob Appleyard with a crowd of 10,000 or so watching and shouting derisively as the ball slipped from my grasp.

As a young player, still making my way, the lapse made me feel sick. I had been punished enough and Bob only added to the pain I felt when, at the end of the over, he came across and rebuked me.

No bowler likes seeing chances go begging off his bowling. But then neither does the fielder enjoy dropping the catch and nothing is gained by the attitude which Bob adopted on that occasion.

Nor was it always fun playing with Johnny Wardle. The crowd thought he was a great entertainer, a real comedian, but some of the younger boys in the Yorkshire team didn't find him so amusing.

I probably dropped eight or nine out of ten chances in seasons 1953 and 1954 simply because I was scared to death of being shouted at by Johnny. The situation became ridiculous because I had always been a fairly reliable catcher and there I was, praying that the ball didn't come my way. Ultimately, I used some native bluntness to Johnny and the tension eased. I clung on to 30 or so catches in the outfield after that.

As I say, I was only a youngster at the time and I can only

assume that the behaviour of Bob and Johnny was symptomatic of the pressures which faced players of their class. Other men of different temperament react differently but, clearly, to those sensitively poised on the fringes of the first-class game, such dressings down in front of the rest of the team can do harm.

Even without the chastening experiences I have described, I reckon it takes at least three years for a player to develop in county cricket. You may come in for your first year and make plenty of runs, but bowlers are also thinking at the same time. They see you play for the first time and they take note of your weaknesses. The second time round they try you out. Maybe you are leg stump, maybe off stump. One batsman plays the ball squarer than another; one plays it straighter. Each batsman's technique is digested and by the third year the bowler generally knows whether that player has learned his craft.

Over the years I have built up a mental card index of the various batsmen and, like any other bowler, I have my own 'rabbits'—those I seem to be able to cast a spell over. Arthur Morris, the great Australian left-hander, was generally reckoned to be Alec Bedser's 'bunny', and there are many other examples.

Some batsmen have these little weaknesses of technique, others of temperament. I know myself, when batting, that so-and-so has got me out several times in past meetings and I have to conquer the nagging doubts in my own mind that he will deceive me again.

4

Touring, and I get 'fined' £50

Apart from the first time one is chosen to play for England, there can surely be few greater thrills for most county cricketers than to be selected for a major M.C.C. tour.

I made my first such trip—under the captaincy of Peter May—to the West Indies in the winter of 1959–60, and quickly discovered that the people of the Caribbean really know their cricket. While I was fielding close to the boundary spectators would illustrate their remarkable grasp of cricketing facts and figures by reciting all the current batting and bowling figures of the M.C.C. players. They didn't spare your blushes, either! At one period during the tour I had not been doing very well with the bat and one little lad—he couldn't have been more than ten—called out: 'Mr. Illingworth: you had five centuries last season, why don't you get some runs here?'

The wickets are magnificent and certainly encourage batsmen to play all the strokes in the book, but whether such tracks would be ideal for county cricket is questionable. I believe that if we were to play our Championship matches on West Indies-type wickets there would be very little chance of getting finishes in three days.

Undoubtedly it is harder for bowlers to succeed in the West Indies. You must learn to do something different—either to be really quick or to spin the ball.

Socially we were looked after very well—too well, in fact. Approaching one Test Match we had to attend seven official functions in ten days.

That is far too high a quota of engagements when you have been playing five hours a day in intense heat. I know this is a problem not just peculiar to M.C.C. teams. Every team which tours has to meet it, and obviously the more oversea tours one makes the harder it becomes to accept the continual round of cocktail parties.

Yet, equally, I realize they have to be an integral part of tours. The local communities where matches are being staged, would justifiably feel affronted if they were told they could not entertain the visiting team. Most of us players would prefer a considerable cut in official functions, but we know that the future well-being of the game depends on keeping people interested. One of the quickest ways of dousing that interest would be to stop these get-togethers.

We met the usual type of people at the official receptions in the West Indies, and found that, generally speaking, they knew more about cricket than many of those who attend similar receptions in England. There is nothing worse than having to answer a lot of silly questions from someone who doesn't either play the game or understand it. If only these people would talk on general subjects, or about their own jobs, it would make the life of the cricketer on tour a great deal easier.

I felt a much better equipped player by the time I was selected for my second tour—to Australia with Ted Dexter's team in 1962-63. Without delving back into *Wisden*, I think I had bowled something like 1,200 overs that summer and scored quite a few runs—more than 1,000 anyway—by the time we set off for Australia early in September. We flew from London to Aden where we spent a day with the British Forces. It is not until you make such visits that you realize what a lot they can mean to the servicemen and their families who have to live in these difficult areas of the world.

From Aden we travelled on towards Australia, stopping off for a one-day match in Colombo, which we very nearly lost. Funnily enough, it had been very calm on the boat, yet immediately we stepped ashore we were rolling about and certainly in no proper shape to play cricket.

Still, once we reached Australia and found our land legs we were soon enjoying our cricket. We drew the series, each side winning one Test, and the only thing which marred a thoroughly happy series from my point of view was the decision to cut my tour bonus by half. I received only £50. So, too, did Barry Knight and Freddie Trueman.

To this day I have still not been informed why I was 'fined'.

When Sir William Worsley, the Yorkshire County Cricket Club's president, received the official letter from M.C.C. stating that we had lost this money on the tour, he asked to see me.

'Raymond, I can't understand this,' he said. 'I have known you for fifteen years and nothing like this has ever happened. Would you like a personal hearing.'

I told him I would welcome one very much, indeed.

'Right, I will fix it for you,' he replied.

Sir William certainly did his best to arrange a hearing. Several times we were available in London, but the Duke of Norfolk, who was manager of the tour, always seemed to be engaged on other business, and I never did get a chance to learn why the bonus money had been deducted.

Without the official explanation I can only guess the reason. I do recall that at one team conference—I think it was after the fourth Test at Adelaide—the players were asked if they had any views to express. I stood up and told the Duke, who was at the meeting with Dexter and vice-captain, Colin Cowdrey, that I thought we made mistakes in our choice of bowling formations. I then went on to explain where I thought we had gone wrong in our selection of the side.

We had drawn the first Test at Brisbane and won the second at Melbourne by seven wickets. Then we went on for the third game of the series at Sydney. The track there was very brown and to me it just didn't look the sort for three seamers. But the selectors thought differently and we lost by eight wickets. Yet Freddie Titmus took seven wickets for 79 and I am convinced to this day that if we had put another finger spinner in the side we would have beaten the Aussies.

The Adelaide strip for the fourth Test was different again in texture. There was plenty of grass on it, but the selectors decided to play two spinners and I was included, although I was sure that wicket wouldn't take any turn in ten days, let alone five. As it transpired this match was affected by rain and left drawn. Nevertheless, more than 1,200 runs were scored on it.

Ted Dexter did explain to me at the time that I was being brought into the team largely because I was in good batting form and possibly I could be handy for bowling them out in the second innings. Ted's theory held some sense, but I still believe that we would have been far better off playing a third seamer, someone like Barry Knight; who could have batted as well.

Now, to this day, I do not know whether my criticism privately nettled authority. If it did, then why were our opinions sought in the first place? Surely we were expected to speak our minds? Perhaps, too, a difference of opinion I had with Colin Cowdrey at net sessesions upset the management.

We were in the habit of getting to the nets at ten each morning and Colin was not arriving until eleven. Now that is not the way I was used to playing things in Yorkshire. If they said nets at ten in Yorkshire, it was not ten o'clock for some, and eleven for others.

Certainly, it was galling to me, after having bowled for an hour, suddenly to be told that I had to carry on a bit longer for a late-comer. We exchanged a few sharp words over this and somehow we never quite saw eye to eye again on that tour.

Now, as I have explained, I can only hazard a guess at the circumstances which led to the 'fine'. Perhaps the two instances I have mentioned were not the cause, but I know of no other occasions when I might have offended those in charge of the team. Indeed, if I had thought for one moment that anything I had said or done was going to be marked down against me at the end of the trip, I should have sought a personal interview with the Duke there and then. He may not have known his cricket as deeply as some tour managers, but he was always approachable. I am sure I could have talked matters over with him.

We, in this country, have always accepted that justice must be seen to be done. In my case, sentence was passed without the defence being called.

I need hardly emphasize that the worst possible inferences could be drawn from briefly worded announcements which state that so-and-so has had his tour bonus reduced. The player, and often his family, can be the sufferers. Once the rumours start to spread, it is difficult to repudiate them.

People say to themselves: 'Something must have happened. There's no smoke without fire.' Well, I honestly do not know where my particular fire was ignited, and no one likes to feel he has been the victim of a miscarriage of justice.

Maybe it is too late now for the matter to be reviewed, but I hope very much that should similar decisions be taken on future tours, M.C.C. will give the player an opportunity to state his case before punishing him financially.

I have dwelt at length on this issue not because I want to indulge in petty recriminations—I have far too much respect for cricket to pursue vendettas. I have laid the facts bare, so far as I know them, in order to focus attention on a serious flaw in the otherwise admirable tour administration of M.C.C.

Let me stress here that our tour of Australia was an enjoyable one. We had many, many laughs, including one or two at the Duke's expense.

I shared a room with Ken Barrington who, at one stage of the tour was having difficulty in getting to sleep at night. He knew the Duke took tablets to help him sleep.

So, early one morning, having tossed and turned on his bed without being able to drop off to sleep, Ken decided to telephone the Duke.

'I am very sorry to disturb you, your Grace, particularly at this hour of the morning,' he said. 'But do you think I could possibly come round to your room and take one of your sleeping-pills?'

The Duke, having only just succeeded in getting to sleep himself after several hours, was not exactly overjoyed at being disturbed by one of the team.

Still, he understood how Ken must have been feeling, and said: 'All right, Barrington. Come round straight away and I'll give you one. That should help you to sleep.' Alas, Ken put down the telephone and promptly fell off to sleep, while the Duke sat in his room waiting for him to collect the tablet.

Long before breakfast-time, news of Ken's gaffe had reached the ears of the rest of us. We doubled up with laughter and had a job to contain ourselves when, at breakfast, Ken received a short, sharp lecture from the Duke on the subject of keeping one's engagements!

Cricket's history is laced with rich moments of humour. I recall one occasion when we were playing Gloucestershire at Bramall Lane, Sheffield.

The Sheffield crowd are never slow at letting you know when things aren't going right. Tom Graveney was batting and Johnny Wardle was bowling to him. Tom pushed one into the covers and Brian Close came dashing in to pick up. He missed completely and Tom took a couple. Next ball was slashed into the air and Closey shouted, 'Right, mine, mine!'

and promptly dropped it. By now the ball seemed destined to
go straight to Brian. Sure enough, he pounced on the following delivery as the batsmen set off on a quickly taken single.
Tom, I think it was, still had a yard or so to make to his
ground when Brian whipped the ball back to the wicket.
Unfortunately, no one was backing up and it went for four
overthrows. Everyone—with the possible exception of the
Yorkshire team—roared with laughter at this comedy of
errors. Then as the final titters died away, a big miner at the
back of the crowd roared out:

'And you can't drive a bloody car, either, Close!' Brian,
you may well know, has a reputation for pranging vehicles.

But to return to my earlier comments on the subject of
touring abroad. I suppose the most enjoyable of all my trips
was one organized by freelance cricket writer, Ron Roberts.
It lasted six weeks, which is just about the ideal length, and
took in most of the main places in South Africa—Johannesburg, Cape Town, Durban, etc.

The team consisted largely of Australian and English Test
players, including people like Richie Benaud, Bobby Simpson, Brian Statham, Freddie Trueman and Mike Smith.
The cricket itself was serious because Ron had put us on a
bonus that if we didn't get beaten we would get so much
extra. All the same the play was carefree enough, without all
the tensions which are associated with the major tours.

Ron certainly looked after the players and I believe he
would have made an excellent manager of an M.C.C. side.
His death at an early age was a great loss to the game.

India is one place I would never tour. I have known quite
a few players, English and Australian, who have toured
there and have never been 100 per cent fit afterwards. Frank
Lowson, who opened for Yorkshire and England in the
1950's, used to tell me that he was never the same player
after touring India.

The 'tummy bug' seems to infect so many. Alan Moss, the

former Middlesex and England fast bowler, went there in the early 1950's, yet he still suffers occasional bouts of stomach disorders. They sometimes last for about a month during which time he loses as much as a stone in weight.

Every M.C.C. tour of India and Pakistan is bedevilled by illness. The hygiene and sanitation in these countries is still many years behind our own standards. Their own people probably build up some form of immunity to the various viruses.

For the visitor, it is virtually impossible to avoid picking up some tummy trouble. That is why I cannot blame any of our players for declining to tour in this part of the world. A few hundred pounds are no recompense for the risk of curtailing your playing career.

Geoff Boycott was one of our leading players who told M.C.C. last winter that he did not wish to be considered for the short tour of Pakistan which was arranged when the South African trip was abandoned. I do not know the exact reasons why Geoff pulled out. He stated them to M.C.C. and said they were personal, but knowing Geoff I suspect that part of the decision could have been a natural anxiety about his health. Geoff is one of those persons who go deeply into every single issue. He may well have argued to himself that if he were to catch something in Pakistan, it might set back his career by several years.

Since the war there have always been top names missing from M.C.C. teams going to India and Pakistan. It is a great pity, because they are such cricket-conscious countries who thrive on seeing the great players of the world. But I am afraid many star performers will continue to opt out of this particular circuit until there are much greater health safeguards for them.

I do not think top class players earn enough from M.C.C. tours.

The recently formed Cricketers' Association were about

to raise the whole issue of fees when the South African tour was cancelled last September.

I have never been quite clear how the M.C.C. look at this question of tour payments. On the face of it, they appear to pay you according to the length of tour—three months, four months or six months. To me this is the wrong way of considering a tour.

I think every tour should be classed as a six-months trip because it is virtually impossible for a player to obtain a job for, say, six weeks before the start of a tour and then another for a month at the end of the tour.

Instead of paying £1,000 for a three-month tour and *pro rata* for longer tours, M.C.C. should regard all tours as a six-month contractual agreement between themselves and the player. No player invited to tour should receive less than £1,500, which is not an unreasonable reward for helping to attract enormous attendances, and vast profits. While no one can expect M.C.C. to pay the type of salary which top executives command, their leading representatives on overseas tours are entitled to better rewards.

In a curious sort of way cricket in this country has always seemed loathe to bring into the open such matters as players' salaries and bonuses. Each individual has to argue his case with his own county and there has never been sufficient weight on the players' side, at least until now. The emergence of the players' association should, in the long term, enable the professional cricketer to have one spokesman, rather in the manner that Jimmy Hill was to soccer.

I believe the case of better rewards for the county player has been immeasurably strengthened by the decision to include top overseas stars in county teams. For years counties have been saying that they cannot pay their own players £1,000. Yet all of a sudden they can find £4,000 or £5,000 for a star from the West Indies, Australia or South Africa.

Of course some of these players are better than the English county players but not *four or five* times better. After one season of seeing these 'imported' stars, not even the great Gary Sobers has proved himself so much superior to our own Test players. He finished last summer with 1,500 runs and 80 wickets and rejuvenated Notts. He made them believe in themselves and his very presence gave a tremendous boost to the county's membership as well as to their gates. But if you accept that Gary Sobers is worth £5,000 a year, then surely our foremost players ought, by right, to command at least half that figure.

Unfortunately, there are still English counties who are reluctant to pay realistic salaries. At the time of preparing this book, I know of at least twenty players who are earning more than the senior Yorkshire players. This, to me, is all wrong. Yorkshire have proved the outstanding team in the Championship for the past decade. They have won the title seven times in this period, twice finished second and won the Gillette Knock-out Cup. They are the Manchester United, the Tottenham Hotspur of cricket.

If you turn in the goods, then you should be paid accordingly. If you are not going to receive adequate financial rewards when you are carrying off championships, when can you expect them?

Yorkshire players, I am told, earned roughly £500 annually before the last war, which was something like three times the national average at that time. To be in a similar position today the Yorkshire players would have to be earning around £3,000 a year. Yet they are lucky if they clear much above £1,400.

Nowadays, the county cricketer has to maintain a good standard of dress. In Yorkshire you have to travel sixty miles a day to some grounds, which means that a car is almost a necessity—and you can't run a car much under £5 a week.

B

In pre-war days a Yorkshire player's wage was sufficient to tide him over the winter months, even if he could not find a part-time job. The present-day Yorkshire player has got to work in the winter if he is to make ends meet, and it isn't easy finding employment out of season.

I am now a representative for greetings cards, fireworks and that type of merchandise which we sell to the retail trade. My hours work out quite satisfactorily and my prospects look reasonable. Yet until I secured this post five years ago, I was like a number of other Yorkshire players, struggling to meet all my commitments.

You don't worry about these things so much when you are in your twenties. You think to yourself: I'll find something later on, but once you get passed thirty, you start to worry about the future. With a county as good as Yorkshire you cannot expect to be holding a first-team place much beyond thirty-six or thirty-seven. So, long before the time comes for you to call it a day as a player, you need to have established some alternative form of employment.

If you are lucky enough, as I have been, to receive a benefit, there is the opportunity to put something away for that day. But many county players never receive enough money to set aside a capital sum for their retirement from the game.

5

Why I left Yorkshire

Last summer I spent a number of worried nights before I could bring myself to the decision to leave Yorkshire.

If there had been any way for me to end my career with my native county, I would have taken it, because once you have played cricket for Yorkshire this is the team, above all others, you want to make your life with.

I had played seventeen years for Yorkshire and had grown up with several of the players. It isn't easy to break away from an environment such as that, but everything came to a head when we asked the committee for contracts and fresh financial arrangements for 1969.

I wanted a contract which would offer me security for three to four years, but Yorkshire, for reasons I have never understood, refuse to give their players contracts. They say they are satisfied with a 'gentleman's agreement', which means a month's notice either way. Unfortunately, it doesn't quite work out that way. If Yorkshire give a month's notice, the player has to accept it, but if he asks for his release, they can be awkward and turn down the request on the grounds that the reasons are not sufficient. In that event they can make a player qualify for as long as two years for another county.

We argued that there should be something in writing, giving either party the right of a month's notice, but the committee would not shift from their position.

I knew then that I had to seek my security elsewhere before it was too late. I believe I have three to four years left in the game and, rather than risk the possibility of being given a month's notice in a couple of years by Yorkshire because younger players were coming to the fore, I had to seek a contract outside the county.

That August weekend I discussed all the implications which such a decision involved with my wife, Shirley, and we agreed that I should submit my letter of resignation on the Monday morning.

I didn't expect to hear anything more about it until the Yorkshire committee held their next meeting. I regarded it as a private matter between myself and the club, but about an hour after I had handed in the letter, Bill Bowes came to me in the dressing-room at Bradford, where we were playing Derbyshire, and said:

'I understand you have put in a letter of resignation. Could I have a word with you about it?'

He could see that I looked astonished and I asked him:

'How did you find out about it? Has John Nash [the Secretary] said anything to you?'

Bill replied that Mr. Nash had authorized him to deal with the press about my release.

Quite clearly there had been no time for Yorkshire to call a committee meeting. I was soon to realize that the decision to release me had been taken by the chairman, Brian Sellers, who declared that if I didn't want to play for them I could go.

I still believe there were quite a few of the committee who would have liked me to stay on as a player, but I doubt whether they could have convinced Mr. Sellers. His word seems to be law. Many times he has stated that the club is bigger than the player. I agree with him entirely. I also think, with respect, that the club is bigger than Brian Sellers, which he seems, sometimes to forget.

If he could get this straight, I feel certain he would go a long way towards straightening out the present difficulties over players' finances.

Immediately Yorkshire announced that I was being

released, I began to receive approaches from county clubs and league sides.

They were all excellent offers which included contracts, and they were all above the salary I was being offered by Yorkshire. Even the league terms for Saturday afternoons alone were comparable—or virtually on a par, with the Yorkshire pay for six-days-a-week cricket!

Until the new pay deal for senior players came into force this summer Yorkshire players had to earn too much by incentive. By this I mean that less than half their earnings were paid in salary form. Roughly 60 per cent, in fact, had to be earned by match money and win money, and, as you will appreciate, this is a hard way of making a living.

If you happen to receive an injury, you can lose a great deal of money. In a wet season, too, you can lose money through no fault of your own.

The Yorkshire players felt last summer that while there should be incentive money, three-quarters of the money should be in salary and 25 per cent in incentive bonuses and win money.

Yorkshire are the only county which still does not offer contracts. In this respect they certainly have not moved with the times. After all, they have coaches and they should be willing to back their judgement when inviting players to join them. The ordinary county professional is not making the money which can be earned on the factory floor. I think he is entitled to seek some measure of security in the shape of a contract—and so, obviously, do sixteen of the seventeen first-class county cricket clubs.

Yorkshire are out of step and unless they change their outlook to contracts, I believe they could have a player-drain on their hands. Youngsters coming into the game will certainly want more than a vague 'gentleman's agreement'.

For so long Yorkshire have shut their eyes to the fact that quite a few of the players who join their staff give up good jobs. Geoffrey Boycott was working in National Insurance; Chris Old relinquished a steady post in a bank, and so on. If they were prepared to take a gamble with their future, surely it was not unreasonable to expect that their employers should also take a risk, and give them contracts.

Let's face it, if Yorkshire hadn't thought sufficiently of a player after signing, they could have got rid of him at the end of the three- or four-year contract, or whatever term was agreed between the two parties. By that time the player probably wouldn't have been able to get his old job back. Even if he did, he would have lost three years' seniority with the firm. So who would have been taking the greater gamble?

If I were running the Yorkshire County Cricket Club and last year Geoffrey Boycott had come to me asking for a contract, I would have given him one for ten years. I would have gambled on Geoffrey being worth his place for the next decade. Here is a gifted batsman who is likely to play for England for a number of years.

If football clubs can give players long contracts, as Manchester United have done for Bobby Charlton, George Best and others, I see no reason why Yorkshire as the premier English cricket county, could not give a player of comparable international standing similar security. A cricketer, don't forget, is far less likely to be put out of the game by injury.

Geoffrey is twenty-eight and still on the way up. Once a player gets as far as Geoffrey, he will always be a good player. He may eventually lose his England place, but he will still be a very valuable member of a county side.

I cite Geoffrey because I consider he illustrates the fundamental weakness of Yorkshire's case on contracts.

Yorkshire members may be prepared to stand for some things, but they certainly won't stand for a second-rate Yorkshire eleven. If the pay situation had been allowed to continue, I am sure the committee would have found themselves under scathing fire from many quarters, not least from where it hurts most—the county members.

Once upon a time there were a number of talented reserves waiting in the wings, ready to be beckoned into the county team. But today, with so many other attractions to occupy the rising generation, Yorkshire cannot call on quite the same steady stream of talent.

Those who are prepared to join Yorkshire want to be assured that, financially, it is going to be worthwhile. A young man, possibly with a wife, is no longer ready to play for Yorkshire just for the honour and glory of representing the champion county. He seeks something more tangible in terms of salary and security.

I am very glad, therefore, that Yorkshire have realized it is useless to go on with conditions of service which every other county have long since abandoned.

Now, with their improved terms and greater peace of mind, the Yorkshire players ought to have a bright future. I hope this marks a fresh era of relations between the committee and their players because as we always say up North —when Yorkshire are successful, so, too, are England.

6

My new county

The county clubs which approached me were Lancashire, Leicestershire, Northamptonshire and Nottinghamshire and each one attracted me.

The proximity of Lancashire to my home would have made travelling that much easier. They are a young side full of potential, with a good seam attack in Ken Higgs, Peter Lever and Ken Shuttleworth and a young left-arm bowler, David Hughes, who is only in his early twenties and promises to develop into a fine spinner.

I think the batting looks a little thin, still, but if Clive Lloyd is available and batting in the middle of the order, there is no reason why they should not develop into a strong all-round team, capable of challenging for county honours.

Northants, on the other hand, already possess a strong batting line-up and if I had joined them, I could have supplemented their spin attack of Mushtaq, Steele and Scott.

In considering Notts, I had to recognize the fact that they play most of their home matches at Trent Bridge. Obviously from a spin bowler's point of view this is not the ideal place to go and play. As a leg-spinner it isn't too bad, but as a finger-spinner, I felt that I would probably not take a lot of wickets there.

The offer from Leicestershire was not quite the best I received, but in accepting it I was influenced by several other factors, notably their decision to appoint me captain.

I saw this as a welcome challenge at my age. I had led Yorkshire on several occasions when Brian Close and Freddie Trueman were away and we had generally done well.

I like the progressive outlook at Leicester and I know that the team contains a lot of talent. Graham McKenzie and Barry Knight are two top-class seam bowlers; Jackie Birkenshaw is an off-spinner of obvious merit and the batting looks reasonable.

Moreover, not long after I joined the county, they signed John Loxton, a 21-year-old right handed batsman, who, I believe, is a relative of Sam Loxton, that fine all-rounder who was a member of Don Bradman's wonderful team which thrashed England 4–0 with the other drawn, over here in 1948.

John first caught the eye of the Leicestershire committee when he came to England last summer. He played in second eleven and club matches and, I am told, scored more than 2,000 runs.

He returned home at the end of the season to complete his university studies at Brisbane. Furthermore, he was anxious to acquire more experience in the Sheffield Shield competition.

At the time of writing, I have not seen John in action, but I received excellent reports from Australia last winter of this young man. These were substantiated by John himself when he played for Queensland. He sounded in good nick, particularly during an innings of 125 against New South Wales.

As Leicestershire had already engaged McKenzie, on an immediate registration, it does mean that John will have to qualify by residence for 12 months. That means he will be available next year, 1970, and I understand that he has agreed to play for the county for at least three years.

Of course, I am conscious of the pressures which surround captains in this modern era—the sort of pressures which persuaded Jim Parks and Freddie Titmus to give up the job last summer.

Neither Sussex nor Middlesex had a successful season and I suppose it is inevitable that irritations creep in which can affect a conscientious type of person. Committees start wanting changes in the team and some of these changes don't coincide with the views of the skipper, who is probably best equipped to know the strengths and weaknesses of individuals.

It is from such small beginnings that these pressures mount up. I don't think they are likely to happen when a side is doing well. The trouble in sport today is that managements and spectators expect success, and often are over-impatient in looking for it.

I mentioned a little earlier that I was impressed by the go-ahead attitude of everyone connected with Leicestershire, and, so, too, was my wife.

They showed their attention to detail when Mike Turner, the secretary, very kindly invited us to the members' dinner. When I telephoned our acceptance, he told me he would book accommodation for us at one of the city's top hotels.

When we arrived, we found that not only were we staying at the hotel in which the dinner was taking place, but a suite of rooms had been placed at our disposal. I never received treatment of that kind in all the seventeen years I played for Yorkshire!

In many ways Yorkshire are still years behind the times in their attitude to the players. They are the champion cricket county, but socially they must be very nearly bottom of the list.

Until recently the Yorkshire players have felt very much the poor relations when it came to offering other teams hospitality. Lancashire, for example, have always invited the players in for a drink in the committee room. When Yorkshire play away, the secretary of the home team always arranges golfing facilities or something similar for the players.

Until the Yorkshire players complained in the last year or so, nothing of that nature was provided for teams visiting Yorkshire. Even then the main effort in organizing something reciprocal in hospitality has come not from the committee but from Mr. John Nash, the Secretary.

John Nash, I know, is sensitive to the players' needs. He has done a great deal for Yorkshire cricket in his quiet, firm way, but with this curious reticence of the committee to move with the times his task cannot be easy.

In everyday working life it is frequently the little things which cause the biggest irritation. You would have thought that providing a few seats for the wives of the players, on the balcony, or in a private section of the pavilion enclosure, would be a simple enough operation. Yet at most grounds in Yorkshire, the wives have to sit among the general public. Now if a player happens to be getting a lot of stick from the crowd—and the language tends to get worse, not better, these days—it is not very pleasant for his wife to be right in the thick of it. My own wife used to get annoyed when she heard people a few seats away shouting something derogatory about me, but she has learned to live with it. But for comparatively little cost, it need not be necessary for the wives of players to be placed in such close proximity to the paying customers. A few seats in a small, private enclosure, should be possible at all grounds.

Whenever I discussed this with officials, they seemed to think it was the obvious solution. Unfortunately for the wives, that is where it generally ended, at the conversation stage.

You cannot easily change the habits of a lifetime. Nor, in leading Leicestershire, would I wish to. I want us to play cricket the way I learned it in Yorkshire. I want us to go out there to play positively, to seek victory from the first ball and to keep on playing for a win until, for one reason or another, that is no longer attainable. Then, and then only, should we play to save the game.

This is what I understand to be the meaning of positive cricket, to enter a match believing you can lick the other side.

I hope, in general, to attack the opposition and back the bowlers by setting attacking fields. Naturally, there are times when you cannot have attacking fields on good wickets. But my intention is to keep defensive thinking to a minimum.

It is the same with batting. I think you must persuade your batsmen that to succeed, they must dominate. They must try to keep the scoreboard moving all the time and, if they find themselves getting bogged down a little, to look for the singles. It is surprising how a few well-taken singles can wrest the initiative when bowlers are threatening to get on top.

One of the priceless assets of playing cricket with Yorkshire is that everybody else in the side is a Yorkshireman, bred and born. They have a feeling for the county, an extra pride, if you like. I make no apology if this theme recurs through the book because it has so much to do with the tremendous successes of Yorkshire cricket over the years. Yorkshire have won the championship thirty-one times outright, nearly twice as many times as their nearest rivals, Surrey. Of course, they have fielded great players but, so, too, have other counties. Yorkshire have always fielded, however, that home pride which must have been worth countless runs and wickets to them.

How, then, can I create a similar feeling in Leicestershire, in a side which has been drawn from a wide area? I accept that it may not be easy, though I should stress here that there is no lack of determination among the Leicestershire staff. Already I have sensed the belief that the championship can be won. Mike Turner was quoted during the winter months as saying: 'With the bit of luck everyone needs we could win the championship, the new Player's County League Trophy and the Gillette Cup.' Well said!

Luck, as Mike stresses, is very necessary in all competitive sport. If we can get off to a good start, win a few early matches and establish a place among the leaders, I am confident pride and enthusiasm will be bursting from the seams of our flannels.

I must confess, as I consider this new adventure, that it could offer me the most exciting chapter of my cricketing days—the chance of leading Leicestershire to their first championship title since they were formed more than 100 years ago.

When news of my departure leaked out, the Yorkshire lads were disappointed at my decision, though they understood what motivated it.

Without being big-headed, I think I have proved a useful player for Yorkshire, and whatever happens, the county must miss me a little. From the players' point of view, the absence of any experienced member of the side could weaken their own position. If they are not winning the championship, they are losing money.

One or two of the Yorkshire lads spoke to the committee before I signed for Leicestershire and asked them to reconsider the position. Indeed, they told me that they were even prepared to play on without contracts themselves if Yorkshire had been willing to give me one. You cannot expect better friendship than that.

Reports of my move were already appearing in the newspapers when I reported for the fifth and final Test match against Australia at the Oval last August.

'Four-way fight for Illingworth' was one paper's headline above the story that four counties were interested in signing me.

The news provided the England boys with all the ammunition they needed to fire their wisecracks at me. Basil D'Oliveira, Ollie Milburn, John Snow and the rest, kept saying: 'Here comes the richest man in cricket.' Every time they saw a letter delivered for me, they called across the dressing-room: 'Another big offer for Ray.' Every time the telephone rang, the chorus went up: 'How much is it this time, Ray?'

I can expect plenty more good-humoured banter when Leicestershire go up to Yorkshire. Now, that really should be a great experience, especially if we beat them!

I can imagine the scene when I go out to bat. Brian Close will be standing a yard from the bat and Jimmy Binks will be chattering all the time behind me! I shall know then exactly how the other county batsmen felt when I was wearing a Yorkshire sweater. Jimmy can give you a real working over with his nattering. He and Closey have captured many a wicket simply because Jimmy has kidded the batsman into a rash stroke.

Last summer Brian Luckhurst was playing well when Kent were struggling against Yorkshire. Closey decided to give himself a bowl. Jimmy warned Luckhurst: 'You've no chance now. The first long-hop he lets go, you'll be out. You'll hit it down somebody's throat!' Sure enough, Closey bowled his long-hop and Luckhurst smacked it straight to me at cover. He departed, cursing himself, while Jimmy exclaimed: 'I told you so! You wouldn't listen!'

I'll be looking out for Closey's long-hop and for Jimmy's other favourite dodge. He'll point at Closey standing a yard or so from the bat and say: 'Look at that ugly so and so. You can't bat with him standing there.'

Now it is just playing into Jimmy's hands if you throw your bat at everything. If the ball deserves to be hit in Closey's direction, then hit it and forget the fact that he is standing there. If somebody is striking the ball well and sends it whistling past Closey's head, he will not exactly be dashing in next ball. If you are blocking all the time, he will creep nearer and nearer until he is virtually touching you. He's brave, but not foolish.

Some years ago we were playing Kent at Canterbury. Colin Cowdrey was batting and he complained to umpire Paul Gibb that Close was moving at silly mid-off just before I delivered the ball. The movement of a player so close to the bat was disturbing Colin's concentration. Brian always moves in anticipation of the stroke. When he heard the appeal to the umpire, he told Colin that if he played properly, without using his pads, he wouldn't be able to field there. While the pair were exchanging words, the umpire was saying: 'Are you ready Mr. Cowdrey? Is everybody still?'

7

Close and Trueman

Talk about Yorkshire cricket and I bet it won't be long before you are mentioning Brian Close and Freddie Trueman. They joined the county side at more or less the same time as I did and were always two of the central figures in the team. It is difficult, perhaps impossible, to imagine what it will be like without Fred. Two completely different characters and, obviously, people of such contrasting make-up would clash from time to time. Yet they had one thing very much in common: Yorkshire cricket. Each passionately determined that Yorkshire should be right at the top and ready always to play their hearts out to see that this was achieved.

Away from the tension of championship chasing, Fred was always one to enjoy himself. Stay up late, a pint of beer, talk 'shop' and stay late in bed in the mornings. Brian is not one for burning the midnight oil. He prefers to be up early in the morning and play a round of golf. He's also interested in studying race-form, whereas Freddie is all for going out to do a bit of shooting.

Both tend to be rebels in their way. Fred could never be driven. Say 'Come on, Fred, you're bowling well this morning. I think you can do this chap, keep going, you're all right', and you usually got all you wanted.

Brian has built up a deserved reputation for fearlessness as a fielder close to the wicket. He has taken some tremendous blows without complaining, so it is odd to recall that before he became skipper he was always going down with injuries. Yet immediately he was given the captaincy, he seemed to take all the knocks in his stride and was rarely missing from the team.

The Farsley junior side which won the League in 1946. We were unbeaten for three seasons. I am on extreme right, middle row

My 'find the erk' picture . . . or a century with a difference. That's me, back row, fourth from right, with 99 other 'lucky fellows' during our R.A.F. square-bashing days at Gloucester

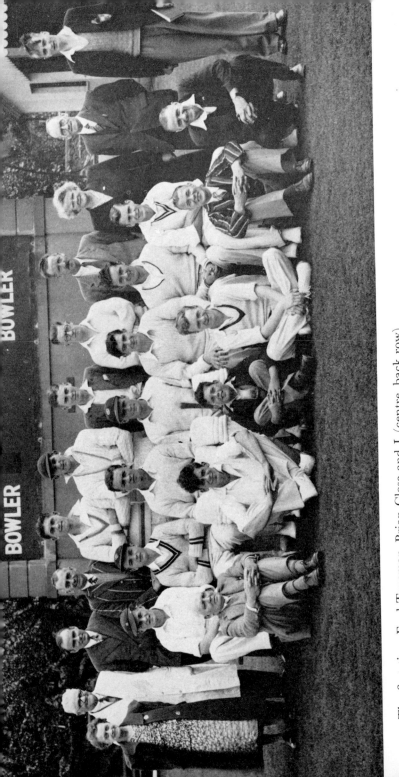

The first time Fred Trueman, Brian Close and I (centre, back row) played together . . . a Yorkshire boys' tour in 1947

With my mother, packing for a coaching trip to South Africa,
1954 . . . and back from sunshine to winter on the Yorkshire moors

Scarborough, 1955 . . . I had just scored the 1,000th century by a
Yorkshire player

In fact, nowadays he tends to get on to the lads when they receive injuries and tells them: 'Come on, you're all right', forgetting how he used to react in the days before he was skipper!

Both Brian and Fred showed the remarkable change which can come over people when they are given the responsibility of leadership. I think it did both of them the world of good, though it is difficult to say which would be the more effective skipper over a long period of time.

Freddie certainly made a good job of it last summer, but it is always easier to come in for the captaincy for a few matches. The real test arises when you have to control players for match after match, season after season, and still retain your enthusiasm. I don't know whether Fred would have had the temperament to stick at the job in a long championship season. He might have found it a hard grind. Fred likes to enjoy his cricket. It would have been interesting to see. . . .

People sometimes overlook the fact that Fred carried a hell of a lot of weight on his shoulders, for a long time and for an astronomical number of overs. I am told he has bowled more than 41,000 overs, a greater tally than any other fast bowler of my time. No wonder he occasionally kicked up a fuss. After such punishment, he needed to let off steam!

One of Fred's biggest failings is that he never knows what time of day it is. That's how he came to be sent home from Taunton in 1962. He had been warned that if he was late again, he would be left out of the team. On that occasion he didn't arrive at the ground until well after the two captains had declared their teams. So Vic Wilson, who was Yorkshire's skipper, announced to the press that Fred was being omitted from the side because he had arrived late at the ground.

What Vic forgot to tell the newspaper correspondents was

that Fred had already received a final warning for un-punctuality. People who didn't know the full facts thought Vic had been needlessly harsh on Fred just because he happened to oversleep that once. Sympathy went to Fred when he didn't deserve it. After all, the rules laid down by successive Yorkshire captains are fair enough. They stipulate that the team should be at the ground an hour before play on the first day and half an hour on the second and third days. No player, however great he is, can expect the rules to be bent to suit his convenience. Fred never did expect concessions. He's just one of those people who can't be on time.

For his part, Brian Close, had a habit of being forgetful. Sometimes when the team fielded badly, Brian would stalk off, telling everyone: 'The fielding was bloody awful today. We'll be down here at ten o'clock tomorrow morning for practice.'

Next morning the team would parade at 10 a.m. only to find Brian was missing! He had forgotten all about his instructions, issued in the heat of the moment the previous evening.

Early last summer Brian caused something of a stir in cricket circles by dropping Fred from a match against Warwickshire at Middlesbrough. Fred was probably not 100 per cent fit at that stage of the summer and Brian decided that as the wicket was wet, he would go into the game with only two quick bowlers. He thought it was an ideal opportunity to give young Chris Old a chance, especially on his own ground, and, I think he was right.

So he told Fred: 'I'm very sorry, but because of the state of the wicket, I'm going to make you 12th man today.'

Not unexpectedly Fred uttered a few choice words, but he soon cooled down. It was the first time he had been named 12th man since he became a senior member of the team, and to such a great bowler the decision must have shaken his pride. I think Fred would have preferred to have been given the match off rather than be made the drinks waiter and the man responsible for locking up the lads' valuables.

Yet he was only being asked to do what all the rest of the Yorkshire team had done in the past. As a matter of fact when Fred is playing he probably has the 12th man running round for him more than any other player!

You try not to make too much of a mug of the 12th man. He is there principally as reserve fielder, but at some grounds there are no adequate security arrangements for the dressing-rooms. So it is then the 12th man's task to collect wallets, watches and other prized possessions and take them to the secretary's office for safe keeping. His only other job is to collect the drinks' order for the end of the day and arrange sandwiches for anyone who prefers to lunch or take tea in the dressing-room.

In recent times Fred paced himself more, but he still shouted and cursed at batsmen. Most of them would probably have thought something was amiss if Fred hadn't called down the Heavens upon them! Yet for the youngster, confronted by Fred for the first time, it was nothing other than an awesome occasion.

To hear Fred talk, you would think he had never bowled a straight one in his life. Everything was pitching leg and hitting off, or vice versa. He will still fume when batsmen edge him.

Last summer Yorkshire were playing Gloucestershire and Fred was skippering. They were nicking him quite a bit off the edge and I suggested he put Don Wilson on at my end and I have a go down the hill. Fred greeted this proposal with a long line of expletives, and then added: 'These so-and-so's have nicked me out of bloody averages.'

Still, both Fred and Brian, were always willing to take advice when captaining the side. They were big enough to appreciate that people like Jimmy Binks, in an ideal place behind the wicket, and senior players like myself, could provide useful information on tactics.

One final anecdote on Fred. Yorkshire were playing the 1967 Indian touring team at Bramall Lane. Rusi Surti, a miniature Sobers, who bats, bowls seamers at the start and then turns to off-spin, was batting. Several times he was struck on the hands by Fred who was bowling fairly quick on a lively wicket. At last Surti lost control and swore at Fred. To everyone's amusement Fred complained to the umpire that a batsman was actually using bad language at *him*!

Now he has left the championship scene. But Fred is by no means finished. He said himself that he was getting out while still at the top and for some years to come he will still play better cricket than many county players can hope to achieve. Well done, Fred, and good luck.

8

Family flights by M.C.C.

I met my wife Shirley while we were still at school, and so by the time we were married she knew all the problems of having a professional cricketer as a husband.

You can spend two and half months away from home in the summer and then, if the player is good enough, there is always the possibility of a further six months away from the family on an M.C.C. tour.

I was away from September to April when I went on the M.C.C. tour to Australia in the winter of 1962–63, which is a long period alone for a woman with young children.

Some players have been in the fortunate financial position of being able to take their wives with them on tour. Peter May, Ted Dexter and Colin Cowdrey have all had their wives on tour, and I think it would be an excellent idea if M.C.C. could help other players in this respect, particularly married men who have been on a lot of tours. If M.C.C. could go some way towards paying the fares for wives to go out to join their husbands for, say, the Fourth and Fifth Tests, it would make the winter nights seem far less forbidding for them.

Frank Russell, who runs the Cricketers' Club in London, does run organized parties to Test Matches abroad. I would like to see M.C.C. arranging something on similar lines. They could obtain a special charter plane at favourable fare terms and fly out wives and several officials for a four-week spell.

I would like to see the *home* Test selectors included in this Family Flight. It has always seemed illogical to me that they seldom see a ball bowled on tour, yet almost every summer they are choosing England teams with winter tours in mind.

For instance, if the selectors had been in the West Indies last year, they would have been in the best possible position to assess the play of Basil D'Oliveira. Most of the critics claimed he had a bad tour, whereas most of the players, including skipper Colin Cowdrey, thought he did quite well, *particularly as a bowler*.

Having played on the West Indian pitches, I happen to know the merit of someone like Basil, who can come on and contain batsmen for half an hour or an hour until the quickies are fresh enough to return.

This is part and parcel of the game out there. You need someone to keep down the run rate until circumstances are right to bring back the heavy artillery. The players who were out in the West Indies assure me that Dolly did that job very well.

If our selectors had seen Dolly at first hand, then I am sure they would have picked him in the first place to go to South Africa, instead of stating they had 'various players who are rather better'.

A great deal of uninformed comment has been uttered and written about D'Oliveira not being a good player on overseas wickets. Surely someone who was brought up in South Africa and played out there for much of his life, should have as much, if not more experience, of playing on these wickets as any of our own players?

I think Basil would have done well out there. Since he has been in our county game he has learned a great deal. When he first arrived on the English scene, Basil was suspect against the spinner. I was able to deceive him in those early days, but since then he has improved his technique enormously against the slower bowlers.

Looking back over the whole of the D'Oliveira furore, it is odd to note that he was actually brought into the England team for the final Test against Australia at the Oval in

August last year for his medium-pace bowling. He was in good nick with the ball at the time, and it was decided that the Oval wicket was no good for three fast bowlers. What was needed was a genuine medium-pacer who might be able to swing the ball, as the atmosphere was heavy during that particular period of the summer.

As things transpired, he did hardly any bowling and scored a magnificent 150. So it just goes to show that you can't always be right in laying pre-match plans.

Basil showed quite remarkable powers of restraint during all the controversy. He is liked by the players, and there was never any suggestion that he should offer to stand down so that the tour could take place.

I know that some players feel that, as a person born in South Africa, he shouldn't be playing for England. Their view is that only those born in England should represent their country and, obviously, they have a point. Nevertheless, so long as the rules permit England to include players born outside the country, Basil had every right to be considered, and no one I have met begrudged him his place.

The great tragedy is that politics should be allowed to interfere with sport. The people who drag it in should keep their noses out. They prevented Yorkshire from going to Rhodesia last year and I fear they will continue to play one against the other. Politicians should sort out their own problems and let cricketers handle theirs. As far as I am concerned the way South Africa run their country is their own business. If they want to send a side here, I'll play them and I'll go there to play them.

I do not pretend to know all the involved background which resulted in the tour being called off. But before proceeding with arrangements for the tour earlier last year, M.C.C. ought, surely, to have obtained a categorical assurance from the South African Cricket Association that Basil would be acceptable. As far as I understand, the South

African authorities never gave M.C.C. such an assurance. Indeed, apparently their only reaction to the M.C.C. request was a formal acknowledgement of the letter.

Clearly, it is a lesson M.C.C. must heed for the future, because almost certainly similar situations will arise, though not necessarily involving the South African cricket authorities.

We might be faced with the West Indies Board of Control not wanting a white South African born player, whom M.C.C. had chosen to tour the Caribbean. Because of the increasing part politics is playing in sport, the West Indies Board, whatever their own views, might have to yield to pressures from outside not to accept the entry of this player because the South African Government had refused to allow Basil D'Oliveira to tour there.

If things go on developing in this tragi-comic way, every international cricket body will be appointing its own Minister for Foreign Affairs.

9

Spinners and spinning

World cricket seems to throw up great specialists in cycles. You will get an era of opening batsmen; a period when fast bowlers command the limelight; a time when all-rounders dominate the international scene. Off-spinners, too, have had their moments, but just now there does appear to be a marked shortage of them at world-class level.

I imagine many people's number one choice at this point of time would be Lance Gibbs, the West Indies star, who established himself as an international performer extra-ordinary when he achieved a hat-trick in the Fourth Test against Australia at Adelaide in 1960–61. Since then he has teased and tormented Test batsmen all over the world and, more recently, our own county players while bowling for Warwickshire.

Yet for all his adaptability to English conditions, I still consider he is seen at his best on West Indies type pitches. He has long fingers and he has learned to bowl a loop-type delivery which gives the ball a greater chance of bouncing on his native tracks. He has quite a fast run-up to the wicket and this helps him to flight his deliveries.

I would say that Fred Titmus is a better bowler than Lance in England, largely because he can push the ball through and he can also bowl round the wicket.

Lance has always struggled to bowl round the wicket. I think this is because he mainly bowls very wide of the crease when he delivers from over the stumps. It means a consider-able adjustment for him if he goes round the wicket, a matter of two or three yards. It may well be that, after a season or two in our county game, he will become more effective bowling round the wicket.

I know he was fed up by the amount of pad play which the England batsmen employed during the M.C.C. tour of the West Indies last year. The obvious answer ought to have been for him to bowl round the wicket to combat this technique, but he seldom did, and certainly not with any marked success.

I have always admired Fred Titmus because he is capable of doing a little bit of everything. He is not the biggest spinner of a ball in the world, but he spins it sufficiently. He can bowl round the wicket. He can push the ball through and he can also flight it. There is not a wicket he cannot bowl on. He has proved this by taking well over 2,000 wickets in a career which he began with Middlesex as a sixteen-year-old schoolboy in 1949. You can't keep taking around 100 wickets a season or more when people have got to know you, without knowing a thing or two about your craft.

I believe Fred would have been an even finer bowler if he was four inches taller. The added height would have enabled him to produce more bounce.

Whenever I think of Fred's bowling, my mind goes back to Sydney, 1963. He took seven Australian wickets for 79 in the first innings and bowled with great skill on a goodish track. He made it turn and also made intelligent use of the wind to make the ball drift.

That, incidentally, was the occasion when England, one up in the series, went into the field with only one spinner, plus Ken Barrington, on a brown wicket. If we had had another spinner, we would have won that match and probably clinched the series. As it was, we lost and Australia went on to halve the rubber.

I am probably a shade quicker through the air than Fred, but I doubt whether there is much difference between us. Fred might have the edge on harder wickets because he may flight the ball a little more. This again is all a matter of what you are required to do for your side. In my days with Yorkshire, if we played on a good wicket which wasn't going to turn, we would use fast bowling with occasional relief spells from the spinners.

Middlesex, on the other hand, have often lacked fast bowlers, especially when John Price has been injured and Fred has had to bowl. That is why he has developed this ability of working batsmen out on good tracks.

I would think I am more effective than Fred on a slow turner, though it is all a matter of opinion and I know that it is never easy to assess one's own abilities. Nevertheless, I was brought up on this type of wicket and I soon learned that to be successful on it you needed to push the ball through. When you have played 17 seasons on Yorkshire wickets which, generally speaking, are slower than most others you bowl on, you certainly ought to know all about exploiting the slow turner!

Gloucestershire have produced many magnificent spin bowlers, not least George Dennett, Cecil Parker, Tom Goddard and Sam Cook. More recently they have been represented by David Allen and John Mortimore, both of whom have played for England.

Of the two, I have always thought Mortimore the better off-spinner, and I know the Yorkshire boys said that if they were given a choice, they preferred to bat against David rather than John.

David has a very slow run-up. In fact, it is hardly a run, and I believe this is the reason why he lacks variety of pace. If you are approaching the wicket a little more quickly, it is far easier to get this variation of pace. John has much more variation and I think he has been unlucky not to play in more than nine Tests, whereas his county colleague, David, has appeared around forty times for England.

The South African, Hughie Tayfield, was a very fine

bowler, particularly on a good wicket. He developed this technique of bowling very close to the wicket, much nearer than anybody else I have known. His arm was actually coming from round the wicket when he was bowling over. As a result, he often made the ball run away to the slips. You thought he was bowling over the wicket at you whereas, because of the position of his arm, he was actually coming from slightly round the wicket. When he was pitching off stump, he was actually missing off, which is an unusual angle for an off-spinner. Normally when bowling over the wicket, he pitches off stump and reckons to get off and middle.

Yet, like Lance Gibbs, Tayfield couldn't bowl his line from round the wicket. He went so wide that he was outside the return crease.

One youngster from overseas whom I have noted down for the future is Ashley Mallett, the Australian off-spinner who is rated the best of his kind to come from Down Under since Ian Johnson. Ashley was one of the surprise selections for Bill Lawry's team over here last summer. He took his chance very well.

In commending him as a likely prospect, I must add a warning that he could develop a throw if he is not careful. He tends to be chest on at the last moment and his arm is a little bent.

He certainly bowled very well against us in the final Test at the Oval, which was only his twentieth game in first-class cricket. I know he won't forget his first Test wicket, a leg-before decision against Colin Cowdrey off the fifth ball he sent down.

Ashley came on just when John Edrich and Colin looked ready to go on the attack. If he had produced a bad over, he could so easily have lost his nerve. As it was, he used his tall, slender frame to give the ball air and, although Edrich, Tom Graveney and Basil D'Oliveira helped England to nearly

500 runs, Ashley finished with creditable figures of three for 87 off 36 overs.

I think, however, that Colin Cowdrey contributed to his dismissal. The wicket was damp on the first morning and we had agreed that if we lost the toss we would try the spinners within half an hour. We felt it might turn. So Colin was understandably apprehensive when Ashley, whom he had not played against, made his second delivery turn quite a bit. He was still trying to decide whether to play forward when Ashley slipped one past his guard. I suspect that if Colin had gone forward firmly and used that first over as a 'sighter', he would not have lost his wicket.

One of the main problems for an off-spin bowler is how to prevent the skin on the spinning finger from getting hard and splitting.

In my early days with Yorkshire I had some trouble, but for the past five years I have kept the finger soft by rubbing in Vaseline so that it skins rather than splits.

In the past I have known occasions when my finger was raw and bleeding from spinning the ball on it. It happened during a match against Surrey at the Oval in the early 1950's. Because of Test calls Yorkshire were without Bob Appleyard and Johnny Wardle, and Brian Close was required for T.A. training. So I bowled all day on the last day and took about eight wickets in some 50 overs. I even got my last two wickets with the new ball.

The rawness developed on the last half-inch of the finger and the longer I bowled, the sorer it became. When play was held up for a time, I thought I would not be needed again. The wicket was greasy and no good for spinners. But the light was so bad that Norman Yardley thought that if he put on a real quickie with the new ball, which had been taken, Surrey would appeal against the light. So he asked me to continue bowling medium-paced seamers, and that's how I got my final two wickets.

All cricket balls are supposed to be the same size to a fraction of an ounce, but, believe me, they are not! I can tell certain makes with the ball in my hand and my eyes shut. That's how much difference there is in size. In fact, because of this variation in size, it does make my grip vary because I haven't got particularly long fingers. If I am given a small ball, then I can hold it with my index finger slightly across the seam. If it happens to be a bigger ball, I grasp it with my index finger up to the seam.

I bowl a genuine off-break, an out-swinger and an off-spinner which I hold a little slacker and it goes straight on. But, of course, all these types of delivery are dependent for success on the various permutations which one must employ —I mean the slower one, the faster one, the one bowled from wide of the crease and so on.

For me the most fascinating part of cricket is this art of spinning a ball.

I know Freddie Trueman, Brian Statham and all the other great fast bowlers will forgive me when I say that any physically strong young man can learn to exploit the seam of a new ball. It requires very much more skill and perseverance to master the craft of flight and spin.

Slow bowling demands thought and infinite patience. If I had to advise a young player how to start bowling spinners, the first thing I would want him to do was to spin ball.

I would tell him: 'Right, lad, you run up, get hold of that ball and start learning to spin it.'

Now I know that many coaches insist that a lad must first learn length and direction. But what happens when he starts spinning the ball? His length and direction go and he has to start all over again.

So my first lesson for an aspiring spinner would be for him to run up and practise, practise, making the ball spin. The action of the hand is rather like that used in turning the knob of a door from left to right.

A spin bowler must depend much for his success on his action. I like to see him standing as straight as possible when he is bowling, and a short delivery stride will help to achieve this.

If you were to study the top spin bowlers, people like Jim Laker, you would notice that the delivery stride is fairly short. This allows them as much height as possible. In addition, by standing up straight, you are able to get the arm action whipping across the body, which gives you that extra spin.

It is important, too, that a right arm spin bowler should get his left-hand side well round and facing down the wicket. It is very hard for a spin bowler to bowl square on, spin the ball *and* get good length and direction. The further you get your shoulder round, the better your action is likely to be.

Co-ordination, then, is an essential ingredient of a spin bowler's make-up. Strong, flexible fingers are necessary too, if the youngster wants to stay the course in the demanding county game.

Once these basic requirements have been mastered, the spin bowler must start thinking how he can lure batsmen into error. He will come against one player who plays off the front foot, another who shuffles back. He must be able to adjust direction that 18 inches or so which can make all the difference between a wicket and a clout to the boundary.

Another batsman will be strong on the offside, or particularly adept at getting the ball through the onside field. Again, it is necessary to adjust the point of attack those few vital inches.

Even after seventeen years or so in the game I still enjoy watching a class slow bowler in action. He is thinking all the time how he can outwit his opponent and I am old fashioned enough to believe that the survival of our game as a spectator sport depends on people employing this tactical and mental approach to their craft.

At the moment, as I survey the county scene, there does seem to be a dearth of spin bowlers. I think of Robin Hobbs and Pat Pocock, both of whom have reached England status, though still quite young, and then there is Geoff Cope who plays for Yorkshire, and Jack Birkenshaw, a fellow Yorkshireman with Leicestershire who could also develop into England material. So, too, could this lad East from Essex, but where are the others?

Yet when I first started in the early 1950's, every side possessed two spinners, most of whom were near international class.

Of all the spinners I have seen in English cricket during this period, I rate Bob Appleyard the best of all. He didn't spin the ball a tremendous amount but it was sufficient at the speed he bowled it. He was an artist at varying his pace— a slow ball, a quicker one and quicker one still which was nearly always a yorker. This made him a wonderful bowler to have in the side in any conditions.

From all accounts he bowled with considerable skill when he went to Australia with Len Hutton's successful team in 1954–55, getting the ball either to bounce a lot or to turn.

We had, too, such characters as Johnny Wardle, Tony Lock, Jim Laker and Roy Tattersall. In my book Jim comes a close second to Bob Appleyard, though on good wickets Roy was as good as, if not better than, Laker.

Johnny Wardle was a great trier. He would never turn it in and was always a valuable man to have in your side because of his whole-hearted attitude to the game.

Another aspect of cricket which has become neglected is leg-spin. We used to have Bruce Dooland of Notts, Jack Walsh of Leicestershire, George Tribe with Northants, Eric Hollies of Warwickshire, Roley Jenkins with Worcestershire, Peter Smith of Essex, and several others.

Leg-spin is the hardest of all to control, but to my mind it is one of the best features of cricket. At least while a tweaker is on, something is always happening. He may get a wicket or he may be receiving a pasting, but the spectator is seeing something positive. Far better that than some of the present-day negative in-swing bowling. That doesn't get the spectator leaping to his feet, except, possibly, in sheer frustration!

Bob Barber is entertainment value when he's bowling in top-class cricket. Take him away and you are probably left with Robin Hobbs and the rising young Middlesex player, Harry Latchman from Kingston, Jamaica.

You then come down to people like Ken Barrington who have really been batsmen all their lives but who can bowl. Ken is a far better leg-break bowler than many people imagine. I believe that it was his ability in this field of the game which tipped the scales in Barrington's favour when the M.C.C. team for South Africa was named last winter. He had not had one of his better seasons with the bat, but had emphasized, on a number of occasions, his potential threat as a leg-spinner.

Harry Latchman impresses me because of his composure when batsmen are getting after him. He possesses flexible wrists, and is not afraid to give the ball plenty of air. If he maintains his current promise, he has an excellent chance of playing for England in the next few years. I hope that if Harry is selected he is spared the considerable mental anguish which Basil D'Oliveira experienced. M.C.C. are due to play in South Africa again in 1973 and though, on the face of it, the two cases would be different—Basil was born in South Africa and Harry hails from the Caribbean—one mistrusts the political and racial interpretations of Mr Vorster's administration.

In my early days I always enjoyed meeting up with 'Bomber' Wells, that perky little off-spinner from Gloucestershire. He was one of the game's characters. The 'Bomber' used to take one stride to the wicket and he could get through an over in about half a minute.

I remember 'Bomber' bowling at me—at Huddersfield, I think it was. The wicket ends were tearing up rather badly and there was a pile of dirt behind the stumps. Unbeknown to me, 'Bomber' plunged the ball into it and when he let go his delivery, a cloud of mud pellets rained all round me!

They have altered the laws since those times and you can't touch the ball on the floor, which, in a way, is a pity. It didn't do any real harm to the game, created a bit of fun and a bit of tension on the field, which kept us on our toes.

Wilf Wooller, who used to skipper Glamorgan, was always up to some subterfuge or other. Yorkshire, with six players under twenty, went down to play at Neath, and Wilf surprised us by taking the new ball and rubbing it on the concrete steps of the pavilion. He made sure he rubbed only one half of it. Then he brought on a spinner at one end and, at the other, used a quickie, making what he could of the bright red half. The umpires didn't say anything. Perhaps they never noticed!

I always liked playing with people of Wilf Wooller's calibre. When he was on the field Wilf was a hard man. He would mutter and grumble at opposing batsmen, trying to unsettle them, and sometimes the air went a shade or two of puce! Yet no matter how tense and bitter had been the exchanges on the field, once play was over he would look into our dressing-room and shout: 'Right, now, I'll buy you a pint.' That's how cricket should be played—hard without recriminations.

Another personality who would do the same sort of thing, was Roley Jenkins, whose rolling gait was such a familiar sight round the cricket grounds in the late 1940's and 1950's.

One day at Worcester all the Yorkshire boys were sweeping him down to square leg. Roley was turning it and that was the only way you could hit him. You really had to get to the pitch, otherwise it turned so much you just couldn't make contact. As batsman after batsman played the sweep shot,

Roley kept taunting them: 'Can't you b—— play with a straight bat!' Afterwards he was first to pay his whack at the bar, and laughing all the time as he recalled the day's events.

Probably the fastest leg-spinner I've ever encountered was Doug Wright of Kent. The speed at which he used to bowl was as quick as any medium pacer. In fact, he could bowl a genuine bouncer in his range of tricks.

The first time I had to face him was at Dover. I always tend to play a little bit off my front foot and suddenly this bouncer came whistling past my nose. You had no way of preparing for it because Doug used to swing up to the wicket with arms and legs in a whirling motion.

Some experts said he was too erratic, but for all his wayward genius, Doug didn't do too badly. I think he took more than 2,000 wickets, 100 or so in Tests alone at a time when Bradman, Barnes, Morris and company were on the rampage.

I said earlier that there did not appear to be many slow bowlers on the horizon. Their development could well have been impaired by the constant changes to the rules, playing 65 overs and that sort of thing.

I hope now that we are getting some sanity back into the rules, we shall see more scope and encouragement given to the young spinner. At least while the slow bowlers are on, you are getting into the region of 23 or 24 overs an hour. If you score three an over off them, that's 60 to 70 runs an hour, which is certainly a more purposeful rate than the 15 or so overs from the quickies.

When you have played in the first-class game for a long time it is not always easy to think of unfulfilled ambitions. If you are lucky, as I have been, to play for England, tour with M.C.C., help Yorkshire to win championships, you have achieved what most cricket conscious enthusiasts would consider a fair share of the honours.

Naturally, I want Leicestershire to prosper under my

captaincy and I know that throughout the hunting county there is a vast reservoir of goodwill for the club. We want to sustain the recent upsurge in their playing fortunes and with all the players anxious to play their part, I see no reason why Leicestershire cannot remain a real force in the championship. I'll certainly be looking forward to our games with my old county, Yorkshire, because, although I have left them, I still regard the players there as my pals.

On a strictly personal note, I would very much like to complete 100 wickets in Test cricket. At the moment I reckon to have around 70 victims and I hope that changing counties won't affect my chances of being chosen for England. I do not see why it should, provided I produce the right form.

Looking back over a Test career which stretches back to 1958, when I was given my first cap against New Zealand at Old Trafford, I suppose the hardest cricket I have ever played was during the 1959–60 M.C.C. tour of the West Indies.

The West Indies batting was packed with wonderful stroke-makers—Sobers, Worrell, Walcott, Kanhai, Hunte, etc.—and David Allen and I were given the task of stock-bowling. We had to keep down the runs until Trueman and Statham were rested enough to return for another onslaught.

That was sheer physical grind with very little reward in terms of wickets. But we won the series—the first time England had triumphed in the Caribbean—and you can well understand how I felt when Peter May, who skippered the team, subsequently thanked me for the way I had bowled. 'I wish we had had you in Australia on the last tour—I think it might have turned the scales our way,' said Peter.

I sent down nearly 200 overs in those five Tests and took only four wickets at astronomic cost, but Peter, as captain, knew full well that bald statistics can be bad liars of events.

In a team game such as cricket so much can depend on the support you give and receive from the other members. As a slow bowler I have always valued the tremendous assistance I have received from England's wicket-keepers—Godfrey Evans, Roy Swetman, Jim Parks, John Murray and Alan Knott. All of these have kept to me and the morale effect of an electrifying piece of stumping or an acrobatic catch can transform your whole game.

Godfrey could make this impact on me. He was such a bundle of energy. He kept everybody on their toes and he made some astonishing catches, especially at full stretch when standing back. He would have made a first-class goal-keeper, despite his lack of height, because he had an india-rubber quality about his movements.

Of the others the present England wicket-keeper, Alan Knott, has impressed me the most, particularly standing up to the stumps. He has the same timing and footwork which were the hallmark of Evans' work, and he is still improving.

One wicket-keeper who certainly deserves to stand along-side those I have discussed is Jimmy Binks of Yorkshire. Obviously I have seen more of his work than most and I consider him to be the best taker of off-spin bowling in the business. There is a neat, professional air to his keeping and many good judges consider he is unlucky never to have represented England in this country. He did win recognition when touring India with M.C.C. in 1963, but since then he has always been passed over. Perhaps it is because he is a specialist and not a wicket-keeper batsman.

If a bowler may be permitted to pass judgement on a wicket-keeper, I would always assess him on the way he stands up to the wicket. Any first-class cricketer ought to be capable of keeping reasonably well standing back. The class shows when a wicket-keeper is close to the bat.

One of the hardest deliveries to take is the near half volley from an off-spinner which turns quite a lot and goes between bat and pad.

Leg-break and googly bowlers also pose special problems for wicket-keepers. Obviously if a 'keeper cannot determine which way the ball is going, he is less likely to take it cleanly.

In theory it is possible for bowlers to give signals to their wicket-keepers, but in practice it doesn't always work out very effectively. A bowler can be deep in thought as he goes back to his mark and forget all about warning his wicket-keeper. He bowls the wrong 'un and the 'keeper is caught on the wrong foot. No, I believe this form of communication only tends to heighten a wicket-keeper's task.

The safest method is for the wicket-keeper to learn, by trial and, maybe, error, to pick the leg-break and the googly for himself.

10

Yorkshire in the seventies

Yorkshire have always prided themselves and justifiably so, on producing their own players. The youngsters have a fine training ground in league cricket where they develop a competitive spirit. The goal for many of them is the Headingley nets and an invitation to join the county staff.

Yet if Yorkshire persist in refusing to give their players contracts, they may find themselves losing them as finance becomes more and more important. Other counties are likely to offer better conditions, including long term contracts, which the young professional with a family to support, might find hard to ignore.

Of course if money does start to dictate the strength of teams, Yorkshire, who are among the wealthiest counties, could always bid for an overseas star or two.

I know there is a deep-rooted desire throughout the county to keep selection to the home-produced player, and I respect it. Indeed, I cannot envisage any revolutionary changes of outlook on this particular issue for the next ten years, but, equally, it would be foolish to pretend that cricket transfers to Yorkshire will never take place.

Another issue which is bound to come up for discussion by the Yorkshire committee in the next year or so is the question of captaincy. Clearly, Brian Close, who is now thirty-eight, has only a year or so left in the game; and Freddie Trueman is no longer available.

Who then are Yorkshire likely to turn to as their leader into the 1970's? Are they still interested in going back to an amateur captain, or do they want to persevere with a professional at the helm?

The two main choices, I would think, are probably Phil Sharpe and Geoffrey Boycott. Phil obviously has the right background for those on the committee who favour public school credentials. He was educated at Worksop College.

On the other hand, Geoffrey is a world-class batsman who has played against all the great players and, in a comparatively short time, has acquired an immense experience of the game. He thinks deeply about the techniques and tactics of cricket, more so than any of the younger players in the Yorkshire side.

If there is to be another candidate from within the existing playing ranks, it could be Richard Hutton. He went to Cambridge and I've heard whispers that he is fancied in some quarters. But I do not know whether Richard would want the job.

My own choice, if I had to make the selection from this trio, would be to plump for Geoffrey Boycott, because of his complete dedication.

It may be, of course, that the Yorkshire committee will give the job to an amateur. By that I mean someone who is not dependent on the game for his living.

I think a lot of county players would prefer to play under an amateur, provided he can breed enthusiasm by his own performances, particularly in the field. A man like Ronnie Burnet, who skippered Yorkshire a few years back. He was not a great tactician, but he gave the boys confidence in their own ability. He was always willing to listen to the senior players and then sort things out for himself.

I agree with those who consider cricket has lost something by the gradual disappearance of the old-style amateur. He brought a refreshing *relaxed* attitude to his play because, if he did fail, it wasn't going to be set against him by committees at the end of the season.

Today few people can afford to take six days a week off from work during the summer months in order to play cricket. Equally, cricket cannot afford to lose such outstanding entertainers as Dexter, Barber, May and the rest.

The long-term answer which could arrest the flow of these class of players from the game might be to play one four-day match over the week-end. They might then be free to return to the game by taking Friday and Monday off work.

One aspect of the game I have not yet discussed is the press. I am told by cricketing friends in the south that the coverage of county fixtures in that part of the country is very sparse indeed.

In Yorkshire, on the other hand, the county club's activities are very well served by newspapers. A corps of about seven correspondents accompany the Yorkshire team and provide their readers with detailed reports of all the matches, both in the county and on tour.

I do not pretend to know how the various sporting coverage is apportioned in newspapers, but it seems obvious that in recent years the space given to cricket has been whittled down.

Perhaps those responsible have been influenced by the fact that cricket is not attracting large crowds, although Yorkshire continue to be well supported at their grounds.

I think they misread the situation. Although many people today simply cannot afford the time to sit and watch cricket all day, there is a vast readership on the game. If the editorial executives on newspapers doubt that, then they should go round the country as I do during the summer months. Go into any club, pub or restaurant, or wherever people gather, and it isn't long before someone is asking: How did so-and-so get on today? I see Barrington got another ton, etc. People still love the game and want to read about it.

While on this subject I do sometimes feel that when some newspapers do decide to report the county matches, they tend to seek what they call an 'off-beat' angle rather than describe the day's play.

If, for example, Geoffrey Boycott, is out for nothing and immediately goes for a net behind the pavilion, with school-boys bowling at him, that is made their story for the following morning. Yet the players themselves—and almost all those with whom I have discussed this issue—would prefer to open their newspapers at breakfast time and read about the previous day's play.

Cricket certainly cannot do without the press and some of our national newspapers provide excellent daily coverage of the county matches. My only regret is that they seem to be in a minority these days. Too many newspapers believe their readership is satisfied with the scorecard details of the matches. As I have said, I think newspapers are misreading the needs of their cricketing customers.

Thinking out batsmen

Trying to outwit the other chap is one of cricket's never-ending fascinations. I believe it applies more to the slow bowlers than to the faster men. A lot of the quickies (and I exclude the really top flight players) tend to rush up to the wicket and let the ball go as fast as they possibly can. They depend on the sheer pace of the delivery to beat the bat rather than subtler methods which the slower bowler needs to employ.

A slow bowler has to work away at getting his wickets. The first thing I look at when a new player comes to the crease is how he grips his bat. The grip can tell you quite a lot. For instance, if the batsman has his bottom hand very much round the back of the handle, I think to myself, 'Well, this fellow is going to be an on-side player, probably a square cutter—but he won't hit so well through the covers.'

Again, if his bottom hand is more at the top of the handle, I may think to myself that he is going to be an off-side player.

I try to set my field accordingly. For the batsman with the on-side grip, I would probably move my cover-point a shade squarer, leaving mid-off straight and set a few fielders in the mid-wicket area.

For the batsman with the off-side grip, I would move my cover straight to contain those shots. Naturally, it doesn't always work out, but a study of a player's grip will often provide a broad guide as to where he will attempt to get his runs.

You notice other points in a batsman's technique which can sometimes be exploited. When Ted Dexter first came on the scene, he was very vulnerable to the off-spinner through the 'gate'—by that, I mean the off-break which turns into the batsman and goes between bat and pad.

I did take him quite often early on in his first-class career because he did not move his front foot very far. Yet being a good player, he learned to move the leg farther down the wicket to counteract the spin.

Basil D'Oliveira is another very good stroke player, but he is vulnerable to the ball which turns into him early in his innings. I have managed to beat him several times with this ball. If he played forward he would probably avoid trouble but he tends to be looking round on his back foot for runs and I have turned it through the 'gate'.

Kenny Barrington is another type of batsman altogether. He plays very near to his pad, half-forward most of the time. Because of this you are not likely to have him caught at short-leg behind square. Kenny is more likely to get a ball which just wedges between his bat and pad and either just bobs out on the off-side or on the leg-side.

When I bowl at Ken, I like to bring someone up close at silly mid-off. You need a brave man to field there, someone in the mould of Brian Close, and I also have a forward short leg.

I find now that when Kenny comes in, he sets about trying to move these close men. He will probably attempt a sweep or some other shot of a really positive kind and, in turn, he makes me think even harder. That's what I mean when I say slow bowling is a continual process of thinking. Often it requires immense patience and always accuracy, but I have found it a very rewarding art.

If I may pursue this theme of thinking your cricket a stage further, I believe it is one of the chief reasons why Yorkshire are such a fine side in the field. I rate them far better than the recent England sides.

You see, Yorkshire have always placed more emphasis on fielding than any other team in the championship. I know that one or two other counties, notably Kent, are now concentrating much more on this department, and they are already better teams.

Every schoolboy cricketer knows the dictum of holding your catches and winning your matches, yet it still surprises me that so many mature players appear to look upon fielding as one of those necessary chores.

When I was with Yorkshire we used to spend long sessions at night discussing the whole theory of fielding. We considered it time well spent because the various changes in the game's rules and techniques made some of the old-style placings no longer effective.

For example, over the last few years, an enormous amount of pad play has crept into the game against the in-swingers and off-spinners.

This form of play clearly affected my bowling. Whereas I used to get two or three people in an innings caught at short leg, the ball just did not go into the short leg field any more. The ball was either getting a thin inside edge and going on to the pad, and then bobbing up on the offside, or it was simply striking the pad.

So Brian Close and I talked over the whole problem and decided that we would be better to post a silly mid-off rather than two short legs for the 'pad player'. We were the first team to do this and others have copied us. I think Martin Horton of Worcestershire was the first batsman I dismissed with Brian standing about two yards or so from the bat on the offside.

I doubt whether anyone has consistently stood so close to the bat as Brian. I remember Sid Barnes used to crouch four or five yards from the bat at short leg when he toured England with the all-conquering 1948 Australian team under Don Bradman's captaincy. He took a fearful blow from a fierce pull by Dick Pollard at Old Trafford and finished up in hospital.

Mercifully, Brian has avoided that fate, but he has taken his quota of blows on the body.

We were playing Gloucestershire at Bristol one season and Martin Young was batting to me. The ball was around leg and middle and Martin just whipped it away at the last moment. Brian was still swooping in at short leg. The ball cracked him smack on the forehead and flew straight to Phil Sharpe at *first slip* who caught it and slipped it into his pocket.

Martin, who was still looking down the legside, had no idea where the ball had gone. When the umpire called out to him. 'You're out', he was astonished. As Brian said, 'I do all the work and Sharpey gets the catch!'

Brian gets a yard or two nearer than anybody else and his very presence does disturb the batsman, who is less happy about playing bat and pad. He will probably discard this method for a more conventional style.

Dover has always been one of my lucky grounds and it was there that Brian's closeness to the bat persuaded Colin Cowdrey to alter his method in one match against us on a slow turner. In normal circumstances Colin would have been quite willing to play bat and pad to me on such a wicket. As it was he tried to hit me. He made 15 or 20 before being stumped. He moved down the wicket in an effort to by-pass Brian and I turned one past him.

A number of batsmen have suffered similar fates when playing Yorkshire. Simply because we have crowded them so much and forced them to play a game that was not natural to them. We upset their rhythm and they got themselves out.

All players should have something to contribute to the task of dismissing the opposition. Yorkshire have proved, time and time again, that it pays dividends to pool your ideas.

Occasionally, I do forget how a particular batsman plays and someone like Jimmy Binks, who notes so much from his spot behind the stumps, will come up and say: 'Oh, So-and-so, do you remember you did him such a way last year. Try him again this year.'

Clive Inman, now a colleague of mine at Leicestershire, plays the ball going away from him very well. But Jimmy reminded me how I had twice dismissed Clive in one match with a seamer. So I tried again when he faced us the following year, and it worked. I had Clive in each innings.

12

England captains

I have played in thirty Tests and toured with M.C.C. to Australia, New Zealand and the West Indies, but nothing has quite matched the emotion of my first game for England, against New Zealand, back in 1958.

I thought I was going to make my Test debut that season in the second match at Lord's. I was brought down from Sheffield where we had been playing Surrey because Jim Laker was having trouble with his spinning finger.

Unfortunately for me, Jim announced on the morning of the game that his finger was better and he would be all right to take his place in England's side.

I was doubly sorry when I learned that the New Zealanders had to bat on a spinner's wicket. England reached 269 and the poor Kiwis were shot out for 47, the lowest score they had ever made at Lord's. Their innings lasted less than two hours, Tony Lock taking five for 17 and Jim Laker four for 13. Following on, they performed almost as badly, this time being all out for 74.

Happily, I didn't have long to wait for the great moment when I was capped. England had gone three up in the series by winning the next Test by an innings at Leeds where Arthur Milton joined that élite company of batsmen who have scored a century in their first Test innings.

So the selectors, presumably looking ahead, made five changes for the Fourth Test at Old Trafford. They brought in Willie Watson, Raman Subba Row, Ted Dexter, Brian Statham and myself for Milton, who was injured, Colin Cowdrey, Trevor Bailey, Peter Loader and Jim Laker.

Crowds were queueing when we arrived at the ground, but

Left: 1958 . . . and a good reason to be happy. My wife and I had just heard of my selection for my first Test match
Right: On to the field with Fred Trueman . . . and we are clearly keen to get on with it

Cricket in the sun is the best
way to live. The next best
thing I found was sailing in
in the Bermudan sunshine
with Doug Padgett at the helm
and Philip Sharpe crewing for
for me—during the Yorkshire
tour of America

I did not feel unduly nervous as some newcomer might from Essex or Somerset, I had the advantage of having played in front of big crowds for Yorkshire and knew something of the Old Trafford atmosphere on an important occasion from our tussles in the 'Roses' fixtures.

That is not to say I didn't feel some tautness in the pit of the stomach. I think you must always have some tension in your system whenever you are facing up to a particular challenge. Without it, I doubt whether you would have the competitive fire to make a success of your job.

The New Zealanders batted first and from the early phases of the innings, when Freddie Trueman and Brian Statham each captured a wicket cheaply, they were always working hard for runs. The 6 ft. 6 ins. MacGibbon showed as much resolution as any of their batsmen, but it took him nearly three hours to make 66. To add to their worries the New Zealand boys were deprived of their wicket-keeper, Petrie, for England's innings, after he had ducked into a sharply rising ball from Trueman.

The New Zealanders finally made 267. My introduction as a Test bowler had been modestly successful on a pitch better suited to the faster men. I took my first wicket by having Playle leg before and my analysis read: 28—9—39—1.

John Reid kept wicket in the early part of the England innings while Petrie was still recovering from an outsize in headaches. Peter Richardson (74) and Willie Watson (66) did their job as opening batsmen and paved the way for a beautiful innings by Peter May. He took such control of all the bowling that he cracked four sixes and seven fours in an innings of 101 which lasted only 156 minutes. Ted Dexter, who like me was making his Test debut, justified his selection with a thrillingly made knock of 52 (two sixes and six fours) in 85 minutes.

When Peter May declared, the New Zealanders were faced to get 98 to avoid another defeat by an innings. Alas, for them, the weather again set them a horrible task on a drying pitch and they were scuttled out for 85. Tony Lock teased and tormented them while taking seven for 35 in 24 overs. This time my figures were: 17—9—20—2.

Certainly the New Zealand players had no luck with the weather on that tour. To have any hope of matching England, they needed to bat on firm tracks. Instead, they found themselves trying to cope with Laker and Lock, two of the world's greatest spinners, on turning pitches.

When you consider they must draw their players from a population about as large as one of our major provincial cities, it is remarkable that they can produce such fine players as Bert Sutcliffe, Reid, Hadlee, Burtt, Donnelly and others like them.

That was my only Test match that summer and while I had not exactly made an explosive entry to the international cricket scene, I felt that I had done sufficient to be noted down in the selectors' books for future reference.

Peter May, whose innings was one of the delights of that season, was a person I came to admire both as a cricketer and as a person. He was not only a good leader of men but a tough one, which may surprise those who think of him as a quiet, self-effacing type. Off the field he is just that. You won't hear him talking about his achievements, and the pages of *Wisden* are littered with them.

Put him in charge of men on the field and he could be as firm as anyone. I think he learned much of this hardness from playing his early Test cricket under Len Hutton.

Leadership is one of those indefinable qualities. Men react to certain leaders, mistrust others. Perhaps inspiration is the basis of successful leadership. Peter was one of those who made you want to succeed.

When the New Zealanders were trying to fight their way to a respectable first innings total, Peter came across to me at the end of an over and said: 'You're doing all right,

Raymond. Now let's get stuck into the so-and-so's. Let's have the so-and-so's out.' Now that was the language a Yorkshire-man could understand. . . .

Peter showed a facility for dominating bowling *earlier* in an innings than most of his contemporaries. You couldn't get away with bowling the ordinary, the mundane, to Peter because he would smash it all over the ground. He let you know from the start of an innings that he intended to dominate. You just could not afford to be untidy in length or direction when he was at the crease.

He once struck Johnny Wardle for an enormous six at the Oval. It flew over extra cover into the top deck of the stand. You don't often see sixes struck in that direction. It must have required considerable strength as well as timing.

Peter often played splendidly against Yorkshire. I recall an innings of 155 he made at the Oval in 1958. The rest of the side made just over 100 runs and Peter's knock formed the basis for one of Surrey's most emphatic wins over Yorkshire who were caught twice by Tony Lock on a track just suited to him.

Peter didn't fancy the really vicious fast ball which flies round the head, but then I haven't met anyone who does! He played everything else without any noticeable difficulty. He was a handsome driver anywhere from extra cover to mid-wicket and could strike well through mid-wicket.

If he did reveal a weakness it might have been when facing an off-spinner. You had just a chance, and no more, of deceiving him early on by pitching just outside the off-stump and aiming to hit off and middle. Occasionally he tended to play the off-spinner a shade too square and, by so doing, he opened himself up a little. I may have dismissed him once or twice like that but, as I say, you had to catch Peter 'cold'.

I was very sorry when Peter decided to go out of the first-class game, but I was not altogether surprised. He had taken a great deal of criticism, much of it unjustly, from the mass media experts and his health had not been too good. I knew he was establishing himself in insurance in London and as he was probably no longer enjoying the tensions at the top, he sensibly became a week-end club player.

Like all the great batsmen, Peter made stroke-making look so effortless. Batting was an exercise in elegance when Peter was in full flow.

Peter was an ideal captain, hard but fair, and always ready to give his players a helpful word of advice or encouragement when it was most needed.

Ted Dexter was a great fellow. You could talk to him man to man. His one weakness, as I saw it, when he was skippering the side was an occasional lapse of concentration. He had a habit of wandering off into his own thoughts on the field when the play got bogged down and nothing much was happening. It was almost as though he was trying to divorce himself from a phase of cricket which was alien to his nature.

Yet this ought to have been the very time when Ted was planning how to end the stalemate. An unexpected bowling change; a switch in field placings; anything to prevent the game from drifting.

Ted, of course, was a great gambler and sometimes he liked to make a tactical gamble on the cricket field. Indeed, with that little bit of luck every gambler needs to pull off a coup, Ted might have introduced a whole new method of bowling for off-spinners on hard wickets overseas.

On the 1962–63 Australian tour, Ted approached Fred Titmus, David Allen and myself before the state match against New South Wales in Sydney and asked us how we would feel about bowling outside the off stump for a lengthy spell. The idea was to make the batsmen play the ball out on to the off-side instead of the leg-side as many of them do when they are playing orthodox off-spin.

I don't think Fred and David were very keen on the

proposition, but I told Ted I was willing to have a go.

So Ted put his plan into action. He packed the off-side and I directed my attack outside the off stump. It very nearly worked, too. I took five for around 100 and the figures might have been better but for several dropped catches. Ted didn't pursue the plan, which was put into cold storage for the remainder of the tour. I have often wondered what might have happened if those catches had been held in Sydney and Ted had taken his 'O' for off-spinners experiment a stage further in succeeding games.

I said earlier that Ted could strike a ball harder than anybody I have seen, and while writing about him, I have just thought of one particular hit of his. We were playing against an Australian XI at Melbourne during the 1962–63 tour and Ted was facing Tom Veivers. He struck the ball and though it never rose more than 10 to 15 feet, it soared over the sightscreen and must have carried some 150 yards. That was a fantastic shot which only Ted could have produced.

People used to say that Ted couldn't play a long innings. He would make his 60's and 70's and then get out. He disproved that theory once and for all with a superb innings of 180 off the Australian attack at Edgbaston in 1961.

He was an exceptionally fine player of fast bowling. He was fearless, and even when Wes Hall was at his fastest I have seen Ted hook him as though it was the easiest thing in the world to do.

He always wanted to dominate the bowling, and to crack it away to the boundary. Sometimes his impatience cost him his wicket, but he showed the right attitude to the game. People would flock to see him because he was always liable to produce a gem of an innings, even if it lasted only a comparatively short time. In an age when the emphasis is on speed, Ted's swashbuckling approach fitted the crowd's mood. We could do with more like him in the game today.

Nothing is more galling to a team in the field than when

batsmen show no desire to play strokes. Nevertheless, it is up to the skipper—and his bowlers—to do their utmost to persuade them to lose patience and play a wild shot or two. I could not help feeling that, at times, Ted became frustrated by the negative outlook of certain batsmen, and his thoughts would drift to his other loves, golf and horse-racing.

Far better pens than mine have lauded his superb attacking qualities as a batsman. All I will say is that I have seen few, if any, who strike the ball with such punishing force.

Colin Cowdrey is a more complex character. It is true he returned from the West Indies last year a much tougher captain, but as a batsman he still has periods when he surrenders the initiative to quite moderate bowlers. For someone who has played in 100 Tests or so in all parts of the world and dominated the finest attacks, Colin remains something of an enigma.

Everyone accepts him as a wonderful timer of the ball. Yet I have seen him, on excellent wickets, letting himself be pegged down by a bowler whom he was capable of 'murdering' if only he cut loose and expressed himself.

I have bowled to Colin in the nets and every ball I have sent down he has cracked back like a bullet. Now there is a vast difference between practice and match play. Some players can look world beaters when tuning up in the nets and comparative novices when facing competition. In Colin's case, he has proved himself so many times in the torrid atmosphere of Test matches, from Sabina Park to Sydney, that it is always exasperating when he develops one of those bat-and-pad phases. It is such a waste of a great player's talents and a vast disappointment to all those drawn to matches hoping to see him give full range to his strokes.

In the past Colin has seemed almost too diffident a person to bring the best out of the players he led. But I noticed last summer that he was more assertive. He would come up to me now and again and discuss an idea. He did not necessarily take my advice. That wasn't the point. What mattered was that he made me feel I was getting through to him—that we were on the same wavelength. Others, too, remarked that he was bringing them into closer contact with the tactical aspects of the match.

In previous seasons and particularly on the M.C.C. tour to Australia in 1962–63, when he was vice-skipper under Ted Dexter, Colin did not create, for me at least, that little bit of extra confidence which can make all the difference to a player in a tight situation.

Now I come to Brian Close, the other Test captain under whom I have served. Well, obviously, as he was also my county skipper, I know far more about him than any of the others.

Let me say straight away that I enjoyed playing with Brian. He has an aggressive outlook to the game, though like Ted Dexter, he has been known to let his mind drift to golf or horses when the play no longer commanded his interest.

When he is really with it, Brian can be the most attacking skipper in the land. A lot of his aggression comes from the positions in which he fields. He will sit on top of the bat.

On certain types of wicket he made my bowling better than it really was simply by making the batsman think he dare not lift the ball off the floor.

I do not intend to go into the rights and wrongs of the so-called 'time wasting' incidents at Edgbaston which cost him the captaincy of M.C.C. in West Indies in the winter of 1967–68. He set down his defence at the time—and you take it or you leave it, according to your philosophy on how the game should be played. I merely record my view that he played that game, as he has played all the others in a long career, hard and honestly. He is not a man to pull his punches. He speaks his mind and outspoken comment can sometimes offend authority.

Yet as his friend and colleague for getting on for twenty years, I believe Brian won admiration in many unexpected quarters for the sportsmanlike manner in which he accepted the loss of the England captaincy.

Some of his severest critics revised their opinions when Brian subsequently reported the M.C.C. tour in the Caribbean for a national Sunday newspaper. His despatches were full of generous tributes to Colin Cowdrewy, the man who had taken over as skipper, and not a hint of bitterness. A hard man, sometimes an aggressive man, but as straight as a die.

I played under him first at Test level in August 1966, when he was called in to try to lift England off the floor after the West Indies had established a winning 3–0 lead in the series.

The odds were heavily stacked against him. Indeed, there were those who felt it was unfair to saddle him with such a gigantic task at that stage of the season. Closey laughed at these well-meaning folk. He thrives on tough assignments. To him, as to all fighters for apparently hopeless causes, he saw the selectors' decision to appoint him as captain as a personal challege. It was up to him to show that, even at that eleventh hour, England could still teach Gary Sobers and his brilliant band of players a trick or two.

Now Brian may not be the most eloquent of speakers, but what he says he utters with force and conviction. When we were gathered together in readiness for that fifth and final Test at the Oval, he told us that we could lick the West Indians out of sight if we hit them hard from the start. He believed it, and any doubters in our camp soon realized the truth of the statement.

The first omens were not entirely encouraging for Brian because once more, incredibly, Gary Sobers won the toss, as he had done at Manchester (West Indies won by an innings and 40), Lord's (Drawn), Nottingham (West Indies won by 139) and Leeds (West Indies won by an innings and 55).

Even the weather seemed made for the West Indies as we took the field to a scene which never ceases to excite me—a vast crowd in shirt sleeves and summer dresses. Above the roars of applause which greeted us as we made our way past the closely packed members' seats, I was able to pick out a fragment, here and there, from the many shouts of encouragement. A good few were aimed at Brian, wishing him well. One sensed, quite sharply, in those few moments from dressing-room to pitch, that everyone was willing him to succeed. Brian told me later that it made a deep impression on him and only strengthened his resolve not to let them down.

Brian was as good as his word. He hit the West Indies right from the start. Ken Higgs swept through Conrad Hunte's defences with just one run turned on the scoreboards and by the first interval Easton McMorris, Basil Butcher and Seymour Nurse had all followed him back to the dressing-room. The mighty West Indies were 83 for four and there was a bounce in our strides to lunch.

We knew, of course, that while Sobers and Kanhai were still free, anything could happen. Kanhai was due for a major score. In his previous six Test innings of the series, he had had innings of 0, 25, 40, 32, 63 and 45, figures which illustrated fairly clearly that too often he had lost his wicket with a rash stroke or lapse of concentration when apparently set.

This time he got his head down to the job of rallying his countrymen and though Brian rang the changes—he delighted the connoisseurs by bringing on Bob Barber's leg-breaks quite early in the play—the West Indies' fifth pair gradually retrieved the morning disasters.

Sobers played as though there had been no alarms. Wristy cuts, swift-footed pulls and many grand drives earned him runs to all corners, until, at 196, he misjudged one from Barber and Tom Graveney pocketed a comfortable catch in the region of mid-off. Kanhai's soundly executed century, to my surprise, was his first in Test matches in England.

We promptly gobbled up the tail and West Indies were all out for 268.

That left England an awkward period before the end of the first day's play and we were all disappointed when Wes Hall smashed a ball past Geoffrey Boycott's guard with only six scored.

That was nothing to the dismay we felt when a googly from Sobers first thing on the Friday morning deceived Barber and by the lunch break we found we were in a sorrier plight than the West Indies had been at a similar stage the previous day. Five wickets had gone down and soon the awful news was that England were 166 for seven, still 102 runs adrift of the West Indies total. Surely, I thought, as I sat disconsolately on the balcony after being caught for a miserable three, these blighters aren't going to do us again?

The answer came in one of the finest partnerships of defiance I have been lucky enough to witness. Tom Graveney, who had stayed while all around him foundered, at last received sustained support from John Murray, who had been recalled as wicket-keeper after Jim Parks had kept in the first four Tests.

To our delight they resisted all that Sobers could think to hurl against them and by the close on Friday, we were 330 without further loss. Tom was on 132 and John on 81. They were to add another 53 runs before Lance Gibbs, picking up smartly, ran out Tom who had batted with all his customary elegance and authority for 360 minutes. His innings of 165, magnificent as it was, for once did not overshadow his partner's play. John can be the most handsome of drivers, and on this occasion his shots certainly bore comparison with those played by Tom.

The crowd, who had risen in a body to acknowledge Tom's great knock, did so again when Murray was l.b.w. to Sobers for 112.

England were then 399 for nine, a total beyond our dreams in mid-afternoon on Friday and, not unnaturally, most of us expected the last pair, John Snow and Ken Higgs, to beat about them for a few overs before the innings closed.

They did certainly beat about the field, but not for the few overs we had imagined. Having ridden moments of good fortune early in their stand, they proceeded to demonstrate to those of us who had fluffed our parts exactly how to bat.

The longer they went on, the greater became their entertainment. The West Indies tried spin. They tried pace, first without, and then with, the new ball. But nothing disturbed this incredible partnership.

The statisticians were busily searching through the pages of cricket history when, finally, Higgs gave a return catch to young David Holford with England's total at 527. Another three runs and the pair would have surpassed the world Test record of 130, set by R. E. Foster and W. Rhodes against Australia in Sydney during the 1903–4 tour.

Higgs made 63 and Snow's unbeaten effort was 63. The keepers of records told us that Test cricket had never produced a situation in which the last three wickets had added 361 runs. We were not surprised!

'Who are these Boycotts and Barbers?' enquired Higgs, straight-faced, as we congratulated our two fast bowlers.

Alas, there was all too little time to absorb the batting 'instruction' which they were prepared to offer us (at a suitable fee, of course!) in England's dressing-room.

We had hit the West Indies hard, but Brian warned us: We have got them going, now. Don't let them off the hook.

At that John Snow slipped off his sweater, and in next to

no time, with able assistance from Murray, had dismissed Conrad Hunte and Easton Morris. Next Basil D'Oliveira beat Kanhai. 50 for three! They were going down, but Basil Butcher decided that the occasion was right to launch a counter-attack. In less than 90 minutes he hustled to 60 and then, aiming for his tenth boundary, he smacked a ball from me straight to Bob Barber at mid-wicket.

The hutch this time was truly prised. The remaining six wickets tumbled on Monday in two and a quarter hours, and we had won by an innings and 34 runs.

Typical of Close's eager captaincy and direction was the way in which he had Sobers dismissed for a 'duck'. He told John Snow to tempt him with a bouncer and Gary, never one to ignore what he considers a hittable ball, went to hook. The stroke always carries risk so early in an innings when the eyes are still adjusting. Brian knew this and was waiting square in the legside field when the ball dollied to him.

After a series of overwhelming setbacks that summer, England's cricket was on the way back to the top and Brian Close's fighting leadership had done much to set it on the right course.

I have often been asked whether I consider it more difficult to captain a county side than a Test team and it is not a simple question to answer.

Clearly, the county captains have greater day-to-day pressures. They are constantly answerable to their committees, more particularly when things are not going well, and in recent seasons their problems have been increased by the spate of alterations to the regulations governing the County Championship.

When yet another method of deciding the championship was tried out last summer—the third, I think, in successive years—the cynics observed that captains would need to add slide rules and calculators to their equipment. The game's legislators decreed that a winning team would receive ten points for a win and the teams five points each for a tie. No points would be allocated for first innings lead but, in addition to the win points, counties would be eligible for a bonus point for every 25 runs over 150 scored in the first 85 overs of their first innings and a point for every two wickets taken in those 85 overs when they were fielding.

That dizzy list of what you could and what you couldn't earn was sufficient to send a few captains for cold towels to press on fevered brows!

13

Other captains

No captain in my time has impressed me more than Richie Benaud.

I experienced his leadership at first hand when he skippered a Commonwealth team to South Africa, which had been raised by the late Ron Roberts, a well-known freelance sports writer and cricket enthusiast.

Richie had that gift of making you feel you were a better player than you really were. He made his players believe they could win, even when the cause looked utterly hopeless.

He was a player of considerable natural talents and so he started with an advantage. People respected him for his ability as a leg-spin bowler, dashing batsman and fine fielder. But he was also an excellent reader of a game and of individual batsmen. He possessed the knack of making just the right bowling change at the right moment. He could size up a batsman's frailties as quickly as any captain I have known, and he knew how to take advantage of them.

Nothing illustrated more clearly Richie's adroit handling of men than his leadership of the 1961 Australian team which came to Britain. They should never have won the rubber with those players, but Richie instilled into them this belief in themselves—this attitude that 'there is nothing we cannot achieve if we set our minds to it'.

Last summer I discussed Richie with Bill Lawry who knows him far better than I do. Bill summed up Richie's captaincy in these words: 'He breathed confidence.'

I doubt whether Bill Lawry, for all his dry humour and friendly manner, could ever create the same aura of assurance. He is a little too defensive in make-up, both as a batsman and as a skipper, as we saw last season when the Test series was drawn.

I am sure Bill came here with the thought in mind: England are the best team in the world after beating the West Indies in the West Indies. I have a young side, a number of whom are fresh to English conditions. We shall be satisfied to contain England. We have only to share the rubber to keep the Ashes.

You might have expected Bill to change his outlook after Australia had unexpectedly won the first Test, but he went on playing it tight. His fast bowlers bowled to three or four men each side of the wicket, saving one, and they tended to bowl short of a length for most of the series.

Even at Headingley, where he was not captain because of injury, Bill still directed Barry Jarman's tactics from the pavilion. The Aussies could have won that match if they had displayed a more aggressive streak. Instead, they made no positive attempt.

I know this negative approach did not satisfy all their players. When I asked Bob Cowper, that fine all-rounder from Victoria, why he had not bowled from the football stand end—the end from which I had bowled—he replied: 'Don't ask me. Why didn't I bowl? It beats me.'

When England batted on the final day, the wicket was turning. I am convinced that had Bob Cowper bowled for an hour or an hour and half he must have picked up two or three wickets. Those would have been sufficient for the Aussies to win the match.

The wicket was ideal for a finger spinner. If England had been bowling we would have won the game comfortably. The Aussies tossed a great opportunity away by timidity *off the field*. You could not blame Barry Jarman. He was only interpreting the instructions and policies of his skipper.

I suppose true captaincy springs from inspiration more

than from a pleasant personality, and sometimes it involves other factors.

When I made my first M.C.C. tour abroad, to the West Indies in 1959–60, the West Indies were led by Gerry Alexander who had won Blues at Cambridge a few years earlier.

He was a likeable man and quite a sound captain. He certainly made us sweat it out after we had gone one up at Trinidad in the second Test. In the end that victory was sufficient to win M.C.C. a series on West Indian soil for the first time.

Yet one sensed that most of Gerry's colleagues in the team and certainly the crowds wanted a coloured chap to lead them. They did not seem keen to be ordered about by Gerry. They had to accept his instructions because he was the appointed skipper, but one felt all the time that they were just waiting for someone like Frankie Worrell to take over. Since then, of course, West Indies teams, both in their own islands and abroad, have been much more disciplined. They have drawn their inspiration from Worrell and Gary Sobers.

Of course, any team which Gary captains is a reasonable one simply because he is playing. He showed this last summer when he took over Notts, who had become very much the poor relations—in playing terms—of the County Championship. Almost immediately he transformed them and they had quite a good season.

Brian Bolus who went to Trent Bridge after seven seasons with Yorkshire, and captained the Notts team a number of times, told me that Gary had done a marvellous job for them.

One of the values of having a player of Gary's talents in the side is the confidence he instils in the earlier batsmen. They know he will be coming in around five or six in the order. So they think to themselves: we can attempt a few more shots because, even if we do make a mistake, there is always Gary to follow.

Gary is an attacking skipper. He is not a man who sets off with a third man or fine leg, and he promotes this attacking image by his own electrifying fielding. I believe he might become a disillusioned cricketer if anyone directed him to adopt a more cautious attitude to his play. Boldness is very much his friend.

I accept that while Gary has been captain of the West Indies he has been able to call upon world-class players to support him. He has had great fast bowlers, marvellous batsmen and spinners.

It could be that any one of the side Gary has led could take over and produce similar results, simply because the talent is there. Personally, I doubt it. Gary is three or four players wrapped up in one. His deeds, when achieved as captain, inspire the others.

Sometime this present West Indies team will begin to break up, if only on grounds of Anno Domini. We may then see Gary's powers of leadership put to fresh tests, but even should they falter, Gary will go on rescuing many situations for his team by those *tour de force* performances which we almost take for granted these days.

When he finally calls it a day, *Wisden*, the cricketers' 'bible', will probably need to prepare a special supplement to list all his astonishing achievements.

I shall never forget having to bowl at him in the First Test of that 1959–60 tour under Peter May's captaincy. We wondered whether his play would be affected by the tragic death of that brilliant young West Indian of the time, Collie Smith.

We soon discovered otherwise. In that Barbados Test, Gary (226) and Frankie Worrell (197 not out) established fresh records for all first-class cricket by batting through two consecutive days' play.

They took the West Indies score from 114 at the end of the third day to 279 by the end of the fourth and to 486 by the

D

end of the fifth. Their fourth-wicket partnership of 399 is second only to the 411 which Peter May and Colin Cowdrey made together at Edgbaston in 1957 for the same wicket.

Both Gary and Frankie were dropped, so you can imagine how we, the bowlers, felt. Glancing again at that match, one of four drawn, I see that Freddie Trueman, Alan Moss and I each bowled the same number of overs, 47!

Gary certainly possesses cat-like reflexes. Neil Harvey, the Australian left-hander, was probably as quick on his feet, without having Gary's all-round talents.

Jim Laker, in fact, maintained that Neil was quicker on his feet than any other batsman he bowled to. Neil could be down the wicket to you before you noticed him.

With most batsmen, I can see them coming and I just pull down the delivery and stop them. The trouble with bowling to Neil was that he left his movement from the crease so late that there was precious little you could do to combat him. He was so swift that he always managed to play it on the full-toss or half-volley.

I had a front view of what was to prove his last big innings against England. That was the drawn Test at Adelaide in January of 1963. I succeeded in bowling Bill Lawry cheaply, but Neil took command in that first innings and made 154. He did little else in the series and at the end of a friendly tour he surprised everyone by launching into a bitter tirade at Ted Dexter. It was an ill-considered and unjustified attack which, in the long term, probably did Neil far more harm than it did Ted.

Stuart Surridge, under whose bold leadership Surrey achieved their outstanding successes during the 1950's, was a skipper who was utterly fearless. He set the highest possible standards in the field and woe betide those who transgressed. He always fielded up close and he would curse the short legs if they weren't right on their toes when the chance came their way.

Surridge was never afraid to give the senior players—
even Laker and Lock in their prime—a telling off, if he
thought they deserved it. He was a lively bowler and could
give it a slog with the bat at the end of an innings.

We had some tremendous tussles with Surrey. Although
a win over Lancashire has always taken pride of place for a
Yorkshireman, victory over Surrey means almost as much.
This has certainly developed from the years when Surrey
were in the middle of their remarkable seven-year run of
titles. The long-standing North *v.* South rivalry also adds
spice to this particular clash.

Surridge always played it hard on the field. Off it he was
a bouncy, jovial chap, ever ready to buy you a drink.

We outplayed them at the Oval during the early days of
his captaincy and needed only about 200 or so to clinch it on
the last day, with the wicket still playing well.

That night it rained heavily. Next morning Surridge
breezed into the Yorkshire dressing-room, grinned broadly
and exclaimed: 'Morning, Yorkshire. It's just rained
enough. You'll find it beautiful out there.' We all knew
Surrey had us on a sticky dog.

I have always had a high regard for Mickey Stewart as
skipper of Surrey. In fact, when I saw him in his first season
in the job—this was in 1963—I thought he looked a future
England captain. Perhaps he might have been given the
honour when Mike Smith was passed over, but I think at
the time he was not in very good run form, at least not
enough to attract the attention of the selectors.

He plays his cricket with plenty of drive and is a thinker
on the game. Once again he is the type of skipper, like
Stuart Surridge and Brian Close, who sets a great example to
his team by his own fielding close to the wicket. There is no
doubt about it that a captain with a flair for snatching up
chances near the bat is at the hub of events. Colleagues and
opposing batsmen are constantly aware of his presence and

that gives a sharpness to the play, which must be good for the game.

Last summer Micky was very unlucky in having so many of his bowlers injured at one time or another. Geoff Arnold and Stewart Storey were two, and he has never really had his two young spinners, Roger Harman and Pat Pocock, striking form together so that he could bowl them in partnership, as Surrey did with Lock and Laker.

Micky's experience illustrates how finely balanced is this whole business of success and failure.

In the three-day county game the skipper is frequently required to make delicate declarations. He must not be accused of setting the opposition an impossible task, say, on fourth innings; equally, he must see to it that his declaration is not handing the points on a plate to the other team.

At least a Test captain is spared the complicated points scoring system of the championship and he does, weather permitting, have five days instead of three in which to decide the outcome of a match. Against that must be set the larger responsibility he must bear in leading his country. In this modern era when every ball is reported on the radio, and television cameras cover large slices of the play, he is under continuous scrutiny. A corps of former Test and county skippers sit in judgement. From their commentary boxes they debate whether he should declare at six o'clock; whether he should take the new ball or retain the spinners; whether the batting order should be altered to meet a changed set of circumstances. The newspaper correspondents, too, add their assessments, and woe betide the skipper who blunders. He can be a hero one match, the villain of the piece a match or two later.

Some men are better endowed physically and mentally to withstand the furious spotlight of publicity, but, even so, captaining a Test eleven is a demanding role.

If I were forced to make a straight choice on the question

of whether it is easier to captain a Test team than a county side, I think I would give my vote to the Test captain. After all, he should have one obvious advantage—the ten best players in the land to lead, whereas a county skipper may have only three or four really top-class performers in his side.

In all these debates and controversies so much hinges on the knowledge of the man concerned.

Len Hutton knew every player who played the game. He saw their weaknesses very early. I saw an illustration of this when I was still a fledgling in the Yorkshire team, playing Gloucestershire.

At that time Brian Close was doing the regular off-spin bowling and he was then spinning the ball more than I. He tended to be erratic, however, and in this particular match, Len saw Tom Graveney coming to the crease at a fall of a wicket.

Immediately, he took Brian off and put me on. As we placed the field, he murmured to me: 'I want you to bowl five maiden overs at Tom. I'm not worried about getting him out. Just try to bowl five maidens for me.'

I would willingly have bowled thirty-five maiden overs for Len if I had possessed the skills, for to me, a lad of twenty and a bit, he was still very much of a god in my eyes.

I did manage to bowl a few maidens to Tom before, to my joy, he holed out at mid-off. Straight away Len came over and said to me: 'Thank you very much', and put Brian back on again.

He had worked out in advance that if I could peg Tom down he would grow impatient and try to break free of the shackles, and we would probably get his wicket. That was one of the first practical lessons I received in thinking out opponents, and I have never forgotten it.

Len, I am convinced, would have made an excellent Test selector, and I would very much like to see someone of Brian Close's calibre being given the job.

He would certainly go for the player with guts, the player who would give him everything all the time. There are no half-measures with Brian. He is either in there doing everything right or, in the case of the Warwickshire 'time wasting' incident, up to his neck in trouble.

The office of Test selector calls for men of special qualities. They must be men you can trust. If they tell you to do something and you do it, and the plan misfires, they must be big enough to admit their error.

Undoubtedly, since I first started playing in Test cricket, the image and attitude of selectors in this country have altered.

When I made my debut in Test cricket, I didn't know who were the members of the selection committee. We were very lucky if we ever saw them during the match.

Nowadays, there is always one or two selectors with us. Personally, I think it would be better if the selectors came in and said 'Good morning, lads, how are you?' and then drifted away, meeting us again at meal-times.

Their presence does not affect me too much because I have played cricket with most of them, and I have got to know them, but I imagine a young lad coming in for his first Test match, must feel on edge, anyway. For him, the tension of the occasion could be increased by seeing the men who picked him sitting in the team's dressing-room or alongside him on the balcony.

After all, it is not as though the team were chosen by one man as in soccer where Sir Alf Ramsey is in sole charge. The England cricket selection committee normally consists of four men. They are all admirable people, deeply devoted to the good of the game, but I cannot help wondering whether their policy of mixing with the players during the sessions when we are batting really helps the newcomers to relax.

One final thought on captaincy. I think now that such

extraneous issues as nationalism and politics are being forced into cricket at international level, M.C.C. should ease an England captain's responsibilities on tour.

He should be in charge on the field and involved in team selection, net practice and that type of thing. But he should not be expected to make speeches at the many functions to which touring teams are invited.

In the past it has sometimes seemed to me that a tour captain has been elected first for his talents as an after-dinner speaker and secondly for his cricketing ability.

The manager should be responsible for speech-making and the skipper for the playing side. The captain's task is to win matches and not to woo diners. He has enough to do working out his tactics without being burdened by thoughts of what he must say at functions.

I have known few, if any, skippers who relish having to entertain guests, many of whom are far better equipped to make the response, for 20 minutes or so. It is a duty which should no longer be expected of them. A brief 'thank you very much for inviting us' is all that need be required from the captain. The main oratory from M.C.C. abroad should come from the manager.

14

Too many cooks . . .

I played my first cricket for Yorkshire as a colt under the captaincy of Norman Yardley. He was then a skipper of considerable experience, both with his county and with England, and to a youngster just feeling his way, he seemed a veritable store of cricketing wisdom.

Unquestionably, Norman read the game well, and tactically he did a great deal for Yorkshire in the field in those early post-war years.

Yet he was not always the strongest of leaders of men, particularly when it came to dealing with such individualists as Johnny Wardle and Bob Appleyard. They required firm handling. Norman was too nice to clamp down when differences arose. Some would say he was too soft.

I can recall several occasions when, say, Bob or Johnny was bowling and Norman would take one or the other off and say to me: 'You bowl the next over from this end.' When my turn arrived, I would move to the umpire's end, ready to peel off my sweater, only to find either Bob or Johnny, whoever happened to be on at the time, already there with the ball in his hand. They would say to Norman, 'I think I'll have another over from this end', and Norman would let them carry on. They would still be bowling many overs later!

Maybe Norman preferred a peaceful existence, but his lack of real captain's authority on these occasions, was out of character with some of the old-time Yorkshire skippers I had read, and been told, about in my youth.

Norman, incidentally, could be a very useful batsman, and at Nottingham in 1947 he helped Denis Compton in a fifth-wicket partnership of 237 against South Africa. That record still stands to this day.

When Norman gave up the captaincy of Yorkshire, his place was filled by Billy Sutcliffe. I think Billy inevitably suffered from being the son of Herbert. Everybody expected a lot of him and he just wasn't in his father's class as a player. Indeed, his confidence must have been undermined by the constant comparisons which were made by the older county members. He might have made a success of the job if he had been a dynamic fielder, but Billy was only average. So he had no chance of setting a spirited example to the rest of the team in the field. Billy was a good sport and I think the committee should not have placed him in a role for which he was not really equipped.

Ronnie Burnet from Saltaire, who took over the captaincy in 1958, proved a tremendous success, though he skippered for only a couple of seasons.

Originally, I believe he was brought in to fire the bullets which were to get rid of the trouble-makers in the dressing-room, but he did far more than that. To me he was the founder of the modern Yorkshire side and everyone in the county owes a lot to him for revitalizing the team at a period when there were discontent and petty jealousies in the camp.

There is no telling what might have happened to Yorkshire cricket if Ronnie had not succeeded in uniting the players and leading them to the championship in 1959.

Ronnie was in his fortieth year when he was given the job and he had never played first-class cricket! That was the magnitude of his task.

What was the secret formula he introduced? I would say the simple ingredients of understanding men and trusting them to do the best they can for the good of the team. If that has a slightly old-fashioned, flag-waving ring about it, I don't care. Ronnie had that quality of winning players' confidences, and it's still a priceless one.

I know they respected him for standing up to Brian Sellers, whereas many others seemed too scared of crossing swords with a man whose word has become almost law in Yorkshire.

Ronnie's decision to give up the captaincy so soon meant that Vic Wilson received an extended term with the county as the new skipper. Vic was a great fellow, 100 per cent for Yorkshire. He rightly expected everyone else to produce the same whole-hearted effort for the county. This dedication, his sturdy left-handed batting and brilliant catching, deservedly earned him selection for Len Hutton's 1954–55 team which regained the Ashes in Australia.

Considering his exceptional talents as a close fielder—though he began in the outfield—Vic may have erred when he became skipper by often posting himself at mid-off. He would surely have made a bigger impact if he had sat on the bat a bit more, close in like Brian Close does today. Captains of lesser talents—I think immediately of Stuart Surridge of Surrey—have demonstrated well enough how they can inspire their team by personal example near the wicket.

Still, Vic worked hard at his captaincy and it could not have been easy for him to stand up to Brian Sellers in the committee room.

One of the disadvantages of being captain of Yorkshire is that you don't have a vote on the team selection committee!

In Yorkshire they have a system whereby about thirteen people are responsible for selecting the team, though probably a quarter or even more do not see more than a few matches each season. The captain attends the selection discussions and for much of the time he probably gets his way, but when the actual selection decisions are taken, he has no vote. Yet really he should have the major vote, the casting vote if you like. He has to run the side and no one knows the players better than he does. You can't spend your working days with colleagues without learning their trade

8

secrets—for example, their ability to play fast bowling; spin the ball; field near the bat, etc.

Some counties have committeemen travelling round with the team, but when Yorkshire are on their southern tour, you can get a situation in which three or four weeks go by without the committee's seeing the team play.

The size of Yorkshire's selection committee is unwieldy. You get people wanting to push players who come from their own area. Officially, of course, they are strictly impartial, but the old rivalries remain between different towns and districts.

The captain certainly needs to be a strong personality to state his case in this cumbersome set-up.

In the past, I have known of instances when people have been sent down to play for Yorkshire and the skipper has been told what order they have got to bat! That is ludicrous. Only the captain should be responsible for the shape of his batting order.

If Yorkshire can't trust the captain to choose the correct eleven and the correct batting order on the morning of the match, then they shouldn't appoint him captain.

That was one of the points I raised when Leicestershire gave me the captaincy. I said to Mike Turner, the secretary:

'I'll take the can back if anything goes wrong. I don't want anybody from outside interfering with the team selection. At least if I make the decisions I must stand or fall by them. Then if you want to sack me at the end of the season that's up to you.'

I think that is a reasonable attitude, and Leicestershire have assured me there will be no more than three people involved, one of them myself. You can expect the chairman of the club and possibly the secretary to involve themselves, but thirteen people is ridiculous!

The trouble with the Yorkshire set-up, while I was there, was that the captain, like the rest of the players, had no contract. He knew that if he got on the wrong side of the committee, his job could be in jeopardy. Equally, if he became a 'yes-man' in the committee room, he was almost certainly likely to lose face with his team-mates. So when Brian Close's future seemed in some doubt last summer because of the pressures placed on him, we held a players' meeting at Bradford. We discussed a number of points, among them improved pay conditions and the introduction of contracts. We also gave Brian a mandate. We told him that if he backed us 100 per cent in committee, we would back him 100 per cent.

We went further. We said we would refuse to play for Yorkshire if they went on interfering with the team. We gave Brian the power of the whole team. We knew Yorkshire could not afford to ignore the united views of the county side.

I hope very much that the committee, at their meetings before the start of the 1969 season, were able to resolve that particular issue with the same good sense as they tackled the players' demands for pay.

Certainly when I left, the players felt strongly that the whole business of team selection and team control needed a drastic overhaul.

15

Coaching

Natural ability, willingness to learn and determination to succeed. These are qualities I would look for in any youngster who came to me for coaching instruction.

Natural ability I would always place first. That is why I think there is a danger in giving a lad too much coaching, particularly up to the age of say, fourteen. If he is a budding batsman, I would let him come to the nets and encourage him to hit the ball, even if his feet were wrong, his stance all awry.

Nothing is more likely to dampen a youngster's enthusiasm in his formative years than to start correcting him for pulling a ball from outside his off stump. Let him *enjoy* the feel of striking the ball. Encourage him to play his strokes, because that, after all, is what batting should be about. Too many lads are taught, too soon, the defensive straight bat.

As he grows up, he should still be allowed to go on hitting the ball, but if he has difficulty in playing a certain type of delivery, that is the moment to help him. After that, it is up to him to practise it. I certainly do not believe in smothering him with coaching advice. You risk creating all manner of doubts in his mind and before you know where you are he has surrendered all his natural attacking stroke technique.

You cannot manufacture a breed of player, at least it shouldn't happen. Everyone is different. The bat is held differently, the feet move slightly differently, even the head is sometimes held differently.

Bob Barber, the Warwickshire and England left-handed batsman, is an example of what I call natural ability. He has this unorthodox streak in his play. He plays a long way from his body, the bat angled for the ball to go through gully, but he's a wonderful striker of the ball for all that. If textbook instruction had been forced upon him in his younger days, we might never have enjoyed his dashing range of shots.

I know some people consider Colin Milburn to be an example of the uncoached player. But to me Colin is reasonably correct in his technique. He certainly pulls the ball better than most because he is so strong but, generally speaking, he strikes the ball in the right direction.

Jim Parks is another who may look wrong by orthodox standards. He does stand square, but if you watch him closely you will see that at the moment of impact he is fairly correct. Immediately he starts to play a shot, he gets his left shoulder round. It is a case of standing comfortably as far as he is concerned and adapting to the need of the particular stroke.

Doug Insole was an unorthodox player. Coaches would have pulled their hair out just watching Doug at practice, let alone in a match. He used to whack them off the stumps down to square leg, but his methods were successful enough. He hit 54 centuries. If you had coached Doug, I think he would have struggled as a batsman, and the game would have been the poorer.

Clive Inman, who is with my new county, Leicestershire, is a little unorthodox, yet he may not appear so from the edge. It is only when you bowl at him that you realize this.

I can bowl to Clive, pitching just outside his leg stump, and he'll still hit it through the covers. He gets really inside the ball and hits it through the offside.

I suppose Bill Alley is another who doesn't exactly conform to the coaching manual on batsmanship. He cuts and carves them around. I wouldn't have thought Bill received any coaching. I imagine he just picked up a bat and hit the ball and found he could do it quite well.

Coaches should just be there in an advisory capacity. They

should never attempt to make a lad change his natural style. There must be a little bit of unorthodoxy in every batsman. Some people open the face of the bat and strike it a bit squarer. Some close the face of the bat, hitting it more on the leg-side. You must have this variation in technique. Otherwise, there would develop a race of players playing strictly according to the text book and it would be comparatively easy to bowl at them. You would say to yourself: Right, I'll bowl a half-volley at the off stump and he'll hit it to mid-off; a half-volley to leg stump and he'll hit it to mid-on; a half-volley to middle stump and he'll hit it straight back. You could set your field accordingly. They would never score runs!

16

Yorkshire regain title

The summer of 1959 ended a barren period for Yorkshire cricket. After the championship had been dominated for seven years by Surrey, the title returned to Yorkshire for the first time since they had shared it with Middlesex back in 1949.

The success, under the new captaincy of Ronnie Burnet, surprised quite a few people, not the least of them Brian Sellers in his first year as chairman of the county's cricket committee.

At the start of the summer, he had gone on record as saying: 'I'll be reasonable in my forecast and say we won't win the championship this year. I have every hope that our young side will win in 1961.'

Well, he turned out to be wrong with both his prophecies. We won the title again the following year, 1960, but Hampshire triumphed in 1961. We were to carry off the championship pennant again, of course, in 1962, 1963, 1966, 1967 and 1968.

Yet eight days before Yorkshire clinched that 1959 title, the side were bowled out for 35 by Gloucestershire at Bristol —the season's lowest score.

Freddie Trueman and I missed that particular match because we were required for England's team in the final Test against the Indians at the Oval.

We won that Test by an innings and thus established a record by winning all five Tests of one series. Australia had achieved this against England in 1920–21 and also against South Africa in 1931–32.

Yorkshire became the new county cricket champions at

A happy moment in Australia (1962–3) and a reliable guide at all times in a sportsman's career. When the youngsters stop asking, you know you're slipping. Unfortunately, too many cricketers forget this when they turn their backs on the kids

Left: David Brown, my England fast-bowling team-mate, naturally likes to see plenty of grass. But when he's a week-end guest at my house he has to work!

Below: A break from cricket during the 1962–3 tour in Australia. Tom Graveney, Fred Titmus, myself, Colin Cowdrey and Ken Barrington leaving our hotel in Perth for a day on the golf course

The England side which beat the West Indies at the Oval in 1966
to restore confidence after a humiliating summer. Brian Close led
England for the first time and until the 'time-wasting' incident
against Warwickshire was favourite to lead the M.C.C. side in
West Indies the following winter
The team: *Back row, left to right:* Boycott, Edrich, D'Oliveira,
Snow, Amiss, Barber. *Front row, left to right:* Illingworth,
Graveney, Close, Murray, Higgs

Bowler . . . this fine action study by *Playfair Cricket Monthly* photographer Bill Smith proves one thing: I don't bowl with my tongue in my cheek!

Hove, after one of the most remarkable fast-scoring achievements in the history of the county championship.

The team were actually set to get 218 runs in only 103 minutes. Impossible, said almost everyone at the ground. But the winning hit was struck with seven minutes to spare!

Sussex were bowled out for 311, and this is how the Yorkshire score grew in that feverish, fantastic hour and half:

> 50 runs in 20 minutes
> 77 runs in 30 minutes
> 100 runs in 43 minutes
> 150 runs in 63 minutes
> 200 runs in 85 minutes

The hero in this extraordinary finish was Brian Stott, the Yeadon-born left-handed batsman who had already distinguished himself several times that summer, notably when he carried his bat for 144 through Yorkshire's completed innings of 262 against Worcestershire at Worcester.

With the pressure obviously on full steam from the first ball Brian scored 96 runs in 86 minutes. Twice he sent towering sixes into the crowd. Yet once we thought his dashing innings had ended. With his score in the seventies, he appeared to be out to a superb catch by the Nawab of Pataudi. But the 'Noob', who had been fielding on the edge of the boundary, immediately told the umpires that he had caught the ball *after* it had dropped over the ropes for a six.

Dougie Padgett also played a big part in the final onslaught, sharing a third-wicket partnership of 141 with Stott.

Yorkshire hit those 218 runs off 171 deliveries and thus edged Gloucestershire and Surrey into joint second place.

Sellers underlined the merit of the Yorkshire championship success when he pointed out that Ronnie Burnet had lost the toss in 20 out of 28 championship games that summer. 'That proves that Yorkshire, at least, are the best second-innings side in the country!' added Sellers.

That summer had other happy memories for me. Certainly after three wet seasons it was satisfying to play so many games in warm sunshine. Most of us felt better for it. I know I did in 1959 because I scored more than 1,700 runs and hit my highest first-class score, 162 off the Indians at Bramall Lane, Sheffield. I also took 100 wickets and helped Brian Close in a seventh-wicket partnership of 184 against the Gentlemen at Lord's which, apparently, was a new record for the Players. Such times as these make up for the days when nothing goes right and you begin to wonder whether cricket is your vocation!

I never cease to marvel at the number of records and personal milestones which are achieved in cricket.

Scarcely a week seems to go by each season without a fresh record being established. I wonder sometimes whether so much statistical information is justified. It can take up precious space in newspaper columns when the reader might prefer to be told more about the actual play.

Nevertheless, whether we like it or not, facts and figures will continue to be unearthed by the statisticians. They revel in spotting the unusual and recording it for posterity.

I am reminded of their eternal vigilance by an event in which, unwittingly, I was the principal figure, not so very long after I became a regular member of the Yorkshire county team.

We were playing M.C.C. at Scarborough at the end of August 1955, and in a drawn match of no particular distinction, I scored 138 in some four and a quarter hours. Vic Wilson helped add 128 for one of the wickets. But what I hadn't realized, until the record-keepers pointed it out, was that my century happened to be the 1,000th hit for Yorkshire. Another milestone had been reached! I suppose historically it is of interest to Yorkshire followers. I can tell my children about it and, who knows, one day they may be telling their children that granddad was the man who scored the 1,000th hundred for Yorkshire! Now on to the 2,000th!

I am still trying to achieve the coveted feat of taking all ten wickets in an innings. I say coveted because since *Wisden* first recorded 'all ten' by a certain W. Clarke of Nottinghamshire against Leicestershire at Nottingham, in 1845, it has been repeated less than seventy times in nearly 130 years of cricket.

The nearest I have come to going through an innings on my own was at Worcester in 1957 when I took nine Worcestershire wickets in a single innings for 42.

At the start of the final day's play in that match, I could not see anything spectacular occurring. Yorkshire were still completing their first innings and the wicket had certainly not misbehaved sufficient for me to think that there would be a harvest of wickets in Worcestershire's second innings.

Yet I suddenly found a spot and all at once we realized that the game was wide open. All the Worcestershire batsmen were in trouble, some from the turn, others from their own indecision. Naturally, we did everything we could to heighten their apprehension, crowding the bat and making sudden changes in the field.

I finished with an analysis of 32—15—42—9 and Yorkshire, left to get 67 in an hour, scampered home with seven minutes—and seven wickets to spare.

When you consider there are nine ways of losing your wicket I think a bowler requires not only ability but also luck to capture all ten.

The nine ways of being out, incidentally, are: bowled, caught, handled the ball, hit wicket, hit the ball twice, l.b.w., obstructing the field, run-out and stumped.

I should add that a batsman can also be given out if, when injured, he employs a runner and that runner obstructs the field or handles the ball. So if at any time you are unlucky enough to need a runner when batting, make sure that your 'aide' knows what he can and cannot do!

Incidentally, of all the remarkable analyses, surely none has been more extraordinary than the great Hedley Verity's performance against Nottinghamshire at Headingley in 1932.

Only the previous year, when almost an unknown, he had taken all ten for 36 against Warwickshire at the same ground. Who, then, could have dreamed that he would repeat the feat so soon—and better it statistically?

This time his analysis read: 19.4—16—10—10. Some bowling! Some bowler! I wish I had been old enough to see him. Alas, he was mortally wounded in Sicily as he led his company on an attack in July 1943.

I always remember an instruction I read in the handbook of a car I owned. It said: Always keep the vehicle smart; somehow it will seem to go better for you.

I think the same can be said of a cricketer's equipment. Look after it, and you'll probably be a better player. That is why I have always tried my best to turn out looking clean and tidy. White shirts and well-creased trousers require either a long-suffering wife or a first-class laundry! If you cannot find either, then there is only one thing for it —you must do your own washing!

Boots, too, need regular attention. Considering the amount of time a county player spends on his feet during the season, I am surprised there is not more foot trouble in the game—and I don't mean 'drag'!

Foot powder or talc powder help to stop the feet from blistering. It is important, too, to ensure that the boots are properly studded and the studs kept free of mud.

Obtaining the right type of bat, a long or short handle, is generally a question of trial and error. You cannot lay down any hard-and-fast rule. Don't oil it too often. Many batsmen like to give their bats a sandpapering before applying a thin film of linseed oil.

Clearly, you must have a bat which not only feels right but sounds right. Gloves and pads are not always given sufficient consideration, which is a mistake. A cumbersome pair of pads can interfere with your running between wickets and, indeed, in the playing of shots. Gloves, whether you choose the gauntlet type or those which leave the palm open, need to give you adequate protection. Remember, a poor pair can cost you chipped and broken bones—and weeks out of the game. Pay the best price you can possibly afford for all your equipment. I am sure there is no cheap route to comfort and safety.

The abdominal protector is a must. Never, never bat without one, and I would strongly advise all batsmen who are constantly facing really fast bowling to wear a thigh pad.

17

I pick my best XI

I have played with and against so many fine players since I first entered the game in 1951 that it is extremely difficult to say who would figure in the Best XI of my time.

As a matter of fact, I spent most of one evening preparing the Illingworth International Set. First I jotted down the list of all the possibles—and found it came to astronomical proportions. Next I adopted a more ruthless approach with my blue pencil—and whittled the list down to around thirty, enough, in fact, to pick two Illingworth XI's!

In the 'senior' of these two teams, my first choice is Sir Len Hutton. Technically, he is the finest batsman I have seen—and any modern team would surely be unthinkable without him, just as the great sides of yesteryear would not be complete without the legendary Sir Jack Hobbs and that other cricketing knight extraordinary, Sir Donald Bradman.

To accompany him to the wicket as opening batsman I plump for the former Australian skipper, Bobby Simpson. He gets preference over several others, largely because of his magnificent slip-fielding—and I want my team to hold their catches!

My batting continues with another Australian, the brilliant little left-hander, Neil Harvey, whose running and throwing from deep positions is another reason why he gains inclusion in the Illingworth first eleven.

Peter May, for his elegant stroke play, and Ted Dexter for his general versatility, follow in the order and at number six, I know I couldn't find a more brilliant performer than Gary Sobers. This man is a natural genius, capable of winning matches almost on his own. To see him striding purposefully to the wicket after that opening array of batting talent, would be likely to destroy the fielding team's lingering hopes of making a contest of the match!

I am content to leave the seam bowling in the hands of Ray Lindwall and Freddie Trueman. Freddie gets my vote over his old Test partner, Brian Statham, because he carries that shade more aggression in his make-up. Johnny Wardle and Bob Appleyard will do me nicely for spin and that leaves me with a wicket-keeper. I'll probably surprise a lot of people by selecting Keith Andrew, of Northamptonshire.

Keith played only three times for England—twice against the 1963 West Indies team which toured here, and once against Australia on the 1954–55 tour. Many knowledgeable observers maintained that he should have won many more caps.

I do not know why he was not given greater chances in Test cricket. Perhaps he belonged to an 'unfashionable' county; or perhaps his 'keeping was so quietly efficient that he did not attract attention from the right quarters. Anyway, he goes into my team, just ahead of Jimmy Binks.

So the No. 1 Illingworth line-up is: Hutton, Simpson, Harvey, May, Dexter, Sobers, Lindwall, Trueman, Wardle, Appleyard, Andrew.

I would look no further than Hutton to be my skipper with May as his vice-captain.

Now for the second best eleven of my playing days.

Geoffrey Boycott and Bill Lawry would be my openers—the one, Geoffrey, for his dedicated application, the other for his sheer guts and fighting qualities. Those two wonderful West Indian batsmen, Sir Frank Worrell, alas no longer with us, and Everton Weekes, would be automatic selections, and I am lucky to be able to call upon Denis Compton and Colin Cowdrey to follow them. Brian Statham and Frank Tyson, in the 'Typhoon' mood with which he swept England to their

Ashes triumph 'Down Under' in 1954–55, take the fast bowling roles.

I would entrust the spin attack to Jim Laker, whose finger spin on a 'dusty' or 'sticky' wicket could be devastating, and 'Sonny' Ramadhin. I thought that 'Sonny' used to throw the ball, but as he passed inspection by the umpires, he wins his place. I am happy to invite Godfrey Evans to fill the wicket-keeping position.

The 'Second' team then reads: Boycott, Lawry, Weekes, Worrell, Compton (D.C.S.), Cowdrey, Laker, Tyson, Evans, Statham and Ramadhin.

Two great sides which, in their prime, would be a promoter's box-office dream if they were to meet one another.

Glancing at the two lists again, I think my money would still be on the No. 1 team.

Mind you, if Jim Laker found himself on a crumbling track, anything might happen. How I would have enjoyed his duel with Len Hutton, the master at playing the turning ball!

18

Geoff Boycott

You can be so wrong on first impressions. When I saw Geoffrey Boycott play his early games for Yorkshire, I thought he would never be more than an average player.

I recall watching him in a match against Northamptonshire. He was under some pressure and though he was certainly not lacking in determination, the ability didn't look to be there.

That was around 1962 when he played only half a dozen games or so. Today I rate him as sound a batsman as anyone in England. His improvement in a couple of seasons was unbelievable.

He was always a very able player off the back foot, but until some two years ago we reckoned that if anybody kept bowling half-volleys at him, they would keep him quiet all day.

Geoffrey needed us to keep drumming home that he had the makings of a fine player before he gained sufficient confidence to go on the front foot.

He stands up a little straighter, too, and gives himself more room to play his shots. Previously he crouched down and cramped his scope for playing strokes.

Mind you, he still wants reassuring. Only last season he would come up to me and say: 'Raymond, what do you think, do you think I am a good player, do you think there are many players better than me?'

I would tell him: 'You are not just a good player, you are the best,' and I wasn't just saying it to boost his morale. I believed then, and still do, that he is on the way to becoming a *great* player.

The word dedication tends to be overworked these days and ascribed to people who may be conscientious in their training and studies, but who, nevertheless, are not exactly spending their whole waking hours perfecting their craft.

Geoffrey *is* entitled to the description—a dedicated cricketer, because when he isn't actually playing, he is either dissecting his performance or in the nets ironing out a fault he has noted in his batting.

He analyses his cricket down to the smallest detail. He will examine a wicket and decide not to play certain shots on it. For example, if it happens to be a very fast one, he will probably eliminate the hook stroke. Furthermore, he will tell the bowler what he is doing! 'My time will come, maybe in the next match, when we will get an easy paced one.'

Geoffrey will work on a bowler. If it is a nice, easy wicket, he will call out to him: 'You can't bounce them on this,' and, human nature being what it is, the bowler will react by trying to bounce one. This, of course, is what Geoffrey has been waiting for and he thumps it away for a four or a six. Then he calmly turns to the bowler and thanks him very much!

I have heard him goad John Snow in this way and John is probably as quick as anybody in the country. He certainly works them up a bit, does Geoffrey.

He keeps himself very fit and even watches what he eats, which for a young player, is unusual.

19

A ticket to Dover, please!

Dover is associated in many people's minds with white cliffs, channel crossings and, more recently, hovercraft.

Whenever the name is mentioned to me, I cannot help recalling a couple of days there in August 1964—two of the most remarkable in my playing career. I scored 135 out of a total of 256 on the first day and took fourteen wickets the next day, seven in each innings!

I suppose we all expected a certain amount of fireworks after hearing that the previous match of the Dover week had been a low-scoring affair.

Derek Underwood had taken six for 43 in Northamptonshire's first innings and Alan Dixon went even better when they batted again, capturing eight for 61. Neither county managed more than 144 in the three completed innings before rain ruined the finale.

The pitch was soaked when Yorkshire batted and no one else really looked at ease. Fortunately, Brian Close refused to be shaken by the problems which confronted us and together we carried our fifth-wicket partnership to 110 runs. That was the only stand of any note, as it transpired, in the three innings, and I finished with a six and fifteen fours as my most profitable scoring strokes.

Next day it was Kent's turn to bat on a spiteful track and again I couldn't do anything wrong. They collapsed twice in the day. Colin Cowdrey played two excellent little knocks and Ted Fillary, an Oxford blue, pluckily held out in one innings. For the rest it was a continual procession to and from the pavilion.

My figures for the two Kent innings read:

First innings: 18—3—49—7
Second innings: 29—6—52—7

Curiously, each time the breakdown of dismissals was identical: two bowled, one stumped, one leg before and three caught.

We won that match by an innings and 13 runs. I completed 100 wickets during the match and went on that summer to get 1,000 runs.

Looking back, I notice that I took six for 29 at Dover in 1953 while I was still a colt. So if you see me rubbing my hands at the prospect of a day at Dover, you'll know that I don't want to see the white cliffs, or take a journey across the channel in a steamer or hovercraft. Just lead me to the Crabble ground!

20

Umpiring

In a world of constantly changing standards it is something to be able to state, with confidence, that the quality of umpiring in English county cricket remains uniformly high.

I never cease to be impressed by the composure, good sense and good humour of our umpires.

The players are often flagging by the end of a day's play, yet the umpires, who are an older body of men, are expected to be as alert during the last half of the day as they were during the first.

The players get their periods of respite. The umpires must go on standing—in sharply contrasting degrees of temperature—and watching every ball which is delivered. Not only are they expected to make instant decisions on a variety of often complicated points, they are responsible for the conduct of the game, the state of pitches, the light, fair and unfair play and a host of other issues.

They are expected to bear, with typical British unflappability, those occasional tantrums from bowlers who have seen their appeals turned down. They are, indeed, always in the 'hot seat'. Inevitably, they err, but as one who has sometimes thought I should have been given the verdict against a batsman, I know that, over a season, these things have a way of evening themselves out.

Sid Buller is widely regarded in all quarters of the game. There is an air of authority in the way he carries out his duties. He seems unruffled by the tensest situation and gives the players a feeling of confidence in his judgement.

Charlie Elliott and Arthur Fagg are two others who deservedly hold high places in the umpires' ratings.

I have also been impressed by Ron Lay. He has not yet been invited to stand in a Test match but, from all accounts, I think it will not be long before he goes on to the Test panel.

Hugo Yarnold, the one-time Worcestershire wicket-keeper, is another excellent umpire, and also something of a character in his own right.

He tells us that the reason he is so small is that he fell from a plane during the war without his parachute!

Whenever the subject of umpires is discussed, it is practically certain that one name will crop up—Alex Skelding, that delightful character whose passing we all regretted a few years ago.

Alex, who took up umpiring after bowling fast for Leicestershire, became famous as the figure in the white boots whose moments of pure comedy would enliven the dullest day's play.

I always thought he had a soft spot for the youngster still trying to make his way in the county game. I don't think he made many bad decisions, but occasionally he would lean a little one way when a youngster was batting. It was as though he was thinking: 'It's mighty close—the lad deserves to get away with it. He's only learning. There'll be time to do him when he has got a few more knocks under his belt.'

Sympathetic, kindly and full of mischief. That was Alex. Half the time you didn't know what he was muttering about.

He used to bawl at the crowd behind the bowler's arm to sit down. Often I am certain they couldn't interpret what he was saying but they sat down just the same. They liked him for what he was—a real character.

The stories of Alex Skelding are legion. He once gave the great Australian batsman, Sid Barnes, out leg before wicket at Leicester, a decision which Barnes received with a look of utter disbelief.

When Alex, who had worn glasses since his days as a professional, returned to the pavilion, Barnes wanted to know how many spectacles he carried and the health of his dog.

The two of them were due to meet up again in Surrey's fixture with the Australians at the Oval and Alex decided to drop Barnes an explanatory note. In it he recorded that he possessed three pairs of spectacles, one for sixes, one for leg-byes and one for l.b.w. decisions. He added that his dog was not permitted on cricket grounds.

While the Australians were fielding at the Oval, a dog scurried on to the field. Barnes swooped triumphantly on the animal and handed it to Alex. 'I thought it never came to the ground,' he said.

Alex was never given a Test. Perhaps authority considered he was too much one of the lads. I know the players would have been glad to see him standing on such an occasion.

While I consider English umpires to be first class, there are a number of excellent officials in other countries, though some of them are subjected to needless pressures from their own people.

We all know of those unfortunate umpires in the West Indies whose own lives and those of their wives and families, have been threatened because they gave out a local hero.

This form of menace places a quite intolerable burden on umpires. How can they possibly do their jobs properly in such circumstances?

That is why there is a strong case to be argued for neutral umpires to be appointed in any area where the local officials are subjected to personal threats.

In these days of fast air travel it would be easy to fly a couple of umpires, say Australian, to the West Indies for instance. They could act without fear or favour because, unlike the local umpires, they would not be wondering all the time whether something had happened to their families.

Our own umpires generally start with a notable advantage over most of the umpires in other parts of the world. Most of them are ex-county players. They have been brought up in the first-class game. They understand the day-to-day problems of the players, and therefore they are well equipped to ensure that the game is conducted in an efficient, professional manner.

Yet I am surprised there is no M.C.C. coaching scheme strictly for umpires. In this day and age when it is not always easy to obtain a sufficient quota of umpires for the first-class, second eleven and minor county fixtures, M.C.C. might well explore ways of encouraging more people to take up the job.

Clearly, finance is a big stumbling block. The umpires stand for four and half months, and have to find other employment for the remainder of the year. Obviously, employers are not rushing over themselves to find work for the man who is free only from October to April.

The long-term answer may be a salary to sustain a man during the out-of-season period.

For those who enjoy cricket and are loathe to cut adrift from the game when their playing days end, umpiring could be the answer. Younger men, too, might be attracted to become umpires if the financial rewards were worthwhile.

Most of the present umpires are older men. However fit they keep themselves, their hearing and eyesight must begin to deteriorate as the years roll by. Younger men, offered careers in the game, could establish a thorough grounding while their faculties were at their sharpest.

Cricketing in Hollywood

Touring is a combination of hard work and fun. When the Yorkshire team decided to make a tour of America, Canada and Bermuda in the winter of 1964 it meant a lot of effort from all the players even before the tour got under way.

This tour was not an official one sponsored by the Yorkshire County Cricket Club. We had to raise nearly £3,000 towards the cost of the trip and we did this by writing to industrial firms and individual businessmen and sportsmen.

They rallied round splendidly and we started the tour in New York where we played two West Indian sides on matting wickets laid on gravel!

No one rushed to open our batting and finally Phil Sharpe was given the dubious honour of taking first ball. It shot off a good length and clouted him on the side of the head. The lads rolled with laughter. Phil's face was a study and his gestures to us could loosely be described as 'un-American activities!'

Still, we survived the odd quirks which those strips produced and enjoyed the games.

We did all the customary sight-seeing trips in New York, beginning with a lunch at the well-known Tavern in the Green. We also went to the top of the Empire State Building where the views are breath-taking.

Yorkshire 'exiles' were soon introducing themselves, among them a New York City 'cop'—Frank Hastie from Wombwell. Apparently he had been a motor-cycle cop for some twenty years. He had escorted many internationally known personalities who have visited the city.

They made us very welcome in New York, but I think most of the boys preferred our next stopping-off point, Washington.

We played a British Embassy side, again on matting, and once more we were conducted to many of the best known places in the city. We visited President Kennedy's grave in the beautifully maintained Arlington Cemetery and looked at the White House.

From Washington, we travelled on to Calgary, but there was to be no cricket for us. A snow-storm greeted us in the morning and after lunch it rained!

Cricket interest has grown enormously in Canada during the past decade. M.C.C. and other representative sides from such countries as Australia, Bermuda and the United States, have all toured there.

The Canadian Cricket Association is a progressive body, anxious to develop good facilities and to further the development of the game in the schools. We were certainly impressed by the Toronto ground.

This is run by the Toronto Cricket, Skating and Curling Club. They were, in fact, the first Canadian side at club level to make a tour of England and France.

The pavilion is among the best I have seen anywhere in the world. It houses squash, tennis, curling, ice skating—almost everything.

Toronto, then, is very much a place to visit, particularly if you are a sports enthusiast.

Yet for outstanding beauty give me the cricket ground at Vancouver. This, to me, is the most striking of all those on which I have played, and I am not forgetting such lovely English grounds as Arundel and some of the little grounds in the Yorkshire dales.

The Vancouver ground's backcloth is the Pacific ocean, majestic wooded country, timber huts and even totem poles. We were blessed by wonderful weather with the temperature around 75 degrees, and, as at all other stops in Canada, we were given fantastic hospitality.

I suppose no tour of the States and Canada would be complete without a visit to Hollywood, and we played on the ground named after that great English actor, C. Aubrey Smith.

I have vivid memories of the match we played in that celebrated film city against a Southern California eleven.

They say that most things are larger than life-size in Hollywood, so when it came to my turn to bat I thought I had better do my best to put on a *Stu*pendous Performance.

The Californians had a spin bowler by the name of 'Jim' Batoosingh and I thumped the first four balls of his over for sixes. I believe I would have 'done a Sobers' but for 'Jim'. He decided enough was enough, and dropped his last two deliveries almost clear of the matting. My arms just weren't long enough to reach them!

Altogether I collected twelve sixes and eight fours in a knock of 144. I'm told my last 100 runs came in an hour. Don Wilson helped me in this run riot and we declared at 326 for nine.

Next, Don kept the heat on by teasing the Californians with his slow left-arm spinners He took six wickets for 11 runs in eight overs and our opponents were all out for 65. I think I took two or three at the other end

'Say, buddy, I thought they said your cricket game in England was short of gasolene,' drawled a local, after he dodged clear of one of the six hits.

This ground is a haven for all the English people who settle in the Los Angeles area. They gather there, discuss the game and convert their American friends, most of whom only know cricket as a sport played by their cousins across the Atlantic.

The British actor, Tom Courtenay, was one of the stars who came to see us play. We knew he was planning to visit the ground because Fred Trueman told us: 'Tom Court-enay's coming down to see me, he is a big mate of mine.'

When Tom Courtenay arrived, he knocked at our dressing-room door and asked to see Fred. 'Who is that bloke?' asked Fred. He didn't even recognize him! The lads gave Fred a real ribbing.

The following year Tom came to see us at Lord's. This time he had grown a beard. 'There is a mate of yours want-ing to see you,' we told Fred, who looked across at Tom and enquired: 'Who the hell is that?' Once again poor old Fred hadn't recognized that 'big mate of mine'.

A riding track is laid round the cricket ground at Holly-wood and most of the lads tried their hand as embyro Lester Piggotts. We had a lot of fun before heading back to New York where the Ford company of America took us round the motor show which happened to be on in the city.

The final phase of our tour took us to Bermuda. This is an ideal place to play cricket. The people are interested in the game and the weather, when we were there, was perfect.

The West Indies skipper, Gary Sobers, joined us for this part of the tour. In linking up with our party he created a little bit of history according to those who know all about Yorkshire cricket lore. He was said to be the first non-York-shire born man to play for the county.

We were glad to have Gary with us because playing against the Bermudans on their own wickets, matting on concrete, was no easy proposition.

We had set out for the tour determined not to be beaten. That didn't mean that we were going to subordinate every-thing else to this end. We still played cricket in a relaxed style but, when the chips were down, we were prepared to work hard to stop the other side from winning.

Once or twice we were compelled to struggle really hard. The ball tends to bounce very high on this type of surface. As a matter of fact we generally lost three or four early wickets against the new ball. The fault we made was in trying to get behind the ball which would bounce chest high.

Eventually, we realized the folly of these tactics. So we decided the only way to play on these wickets was to step back outside the leg stump and slash the shorter balls.

If they happened to pitch well up, we were able to move back into the line of the ball.

Nevertheless, while we were still developing the technique, we were given some anxious moments. In the end we won most of our matches.

Huge crowds packed the grounds and I am told they made about £4,000 or £5,000 profit from our tour. At times they must have been taking £1,000 a day in beer at the bars. You should have seen the yard at the back of the bar— six or seven feet deep in tin cans!

The first time I ever went abroad as a cricketer was in 1955 when I accepted an appointment to coach the Christian Brothers College in Kimberley.

Joe Hardstaff, that wonderfully elegant batsman with Nottinghamshire and England, went out with me on the same boat. He had been coach at the local high school there for a number of years and was very well organized.

He used to have a car provided and often spent hours practising his golf-driving. He would hit 50 or 60 balls and a little lad would run around collecting them all up.

I had spent about a month in South Africa when I developed an abscess. It needed an operation, but the wound would not heal properly. After being examined by various doctors, I was told I had T.B.

The news understandably alarmed me because, having played with the Yorkshire side in the 1950's, I could visualize dropping out of the county team as Bob Appleyard had done. Bob missed more than 12 months' cricket and was never quite as good a bowler again.

I spent several months in and out of hospital. The medical

authorities kept taking tests and they were still convinced that I had T.B.

Eventually, I decided to fly home via Rome and Paris. My companions included Alan Oakman, the Sussex all-rounder, and Bill Greensmith, the Essex leg-break bowler, who was born in Middlesbrough.

The weather when we landed in Paris was some of the coldest I have ever known. I recall Alan was such a mass of goose pimples that he kept his pyjamas on under his clothes!

Immediately I arrived home, I went to Leeds to see the specialist who had operated on Bob Appleyard. He just looked at my finger nails and my teeth and said: 'You haven't got T.B. However, we will do a few tests just to convince you.'

The tests confirmed his assurance. You can imagine what a weight was lifted from my mind.

The specialist then took me to see a professor who examined the operation I had undergone for the abscess. He diagnosed what was wrong and explained that I would have to be operated on again.

This time the wound healed perfectly and my worries were over. It certainly made me appreciate that of all the prized possessions open to man that of good health is certainly the greatest.

22

The pick of Yorkshire

What do cricketers do in the winter? When we are not touring or coaching abroad, most of us find other employment, and, in quieter moments, talk cricket!

The very nature of the game lends itself to endless discussion on great players, great moments and that favourite pastime, selecting teams.

When I was trying to shape this book, I wondered whether, having named a best international eleven of my time, I could choose one drawn from Yorkshire players of the same period.

I wrote down the name Hutton without any soul-searching, and Geoffrey Boycott seemed an obvious number two. Frank Lowson, of course, had been Len's partner and I am sorry not to be able to find a place for him because he gave Yorkshire splendid service. He scored something over 15,000 runs at an average of nearly 40 and played for England, but Geoffrey must win preference.

Both Len and Geoffrey can score quickly, especially if they know that there is batting in depth down the order. Each, in his own period, has had the chief responsibility for getting the innings off to a solid start. When once I discussed Len's patient approach to an innings, he replied: 'Well look what was to follow.' He knew that often the batting line-up was not strong and much depended on his own performance.

Finding a number three caused me a lot more thought. Remember, I was choosing a *team*, not just eleven players. I wanted an ideal balance and that meant fielding had to be taken into consideration.

For that reason, I finally settled for Doug Padgett, a selection that may surprise some people. Doug is a good all-round fielder and thoroughly dependable, the type any captain would be glad to have in his side.

I went for Willie Watson at number four because as a left-hander, he gives the batting a little more variety and poses additional problems for the bowlers. Willie is a fine fielder, too. In passing, I hope he makes a big success of his new life in South Africa where he is coaching both cricket and football at the Wanderers Club of Johannesburg. Willie, one of those rare birds, an international at both games, played soccer for Sunderland and Huddersfield, and was a member of England's World Cup in Rio in 1950. It is strange that I should follow him to Leicestershire as captain.

Phil Sharpe earned the number five position because I needed a top-class close fielder, someone to snap up the sharp chances.

Then I turned my attentions to a wicket-keeper. Who should it be, Jimmy Binks or Don Brennan? Both are technically sound, and as batsmen both could produce their forties and fifties. In the end, I plumped for Jimmy, simply because I have seen more of him.

Then I came to fast bowlers and, like Hutton, the name of Frederick Sewards Trueman promptly went down on my list. The other quickie required more consideration before I settled for Alex Coxon. This man was a great-hearted trier who would bowl all day and I had to visualize the possibility of this Yorkshire XI facing a long day or two in the field!

The team is taking shape, though I confess there were a number of screwed up sheets of paper in the litter basket before I reached this far.

I gave the left-arm role to Johnny Wardle because he can bowl everything, and has a greater all-round range than Don Wilson, and I had no doubts about the off-spinner—Bob

Appleyard. He was such a great bowler before he had the misfortune to develop T.B.

That left me with one place to complete the eleven. I decided that an all-rounder would be useful and my vote went to Brian Close who, in his younger days especially, could also use the new ball effectively.

So this is how the best Yorkshire team of my time eventually emerged: Hutton, Boycott, Padgett, Watson, Sharpe, Close, Binks, Appleyard, Trueman, Wardle and Coxon.

As I scrutinized the list I felt only one cause for dissatisfaction. It was not such a good fielding combination as the Yorkshire side I left at the end of last season. If I could have squeezed a place for Ken Taylor, I would certainly have done so because he was such an asset at cover.

I showed the list to my wife and she asked whom I was nominating as twelfth man. Fair point! I hadn't made provision for one. I put Frank Lowson's name down in case we needed an extra batsman.

All that was left for me to do was to appoint a skipper. Len Hutton had led England when the Ashes were recovered; Willie Watson had skippered Leicestershire, but as it was a Yorkshire team, I decided to name Brian Close. After all, he was the only one of the three who was an officially elected captain of the county.

Somehow I think Closey would have relished handling a team of that potential!

23

Those 'Roses' games

When I first started playing for Yorkshire against Lancashire in the early 1950's, there was certainly more tension between the teams than exists today.

The players didn't speak to each other very much. In fact, it has been observed that all we used to say was 'How's that?' and 'Goodbye!' when the player was out. Of course, I realize that since those days I have matured. I am no longer a new boy among a lot of senior professionals. The youngsters who come into these 'Roses' fixtures still find them very tough, demanding games, but for all that, I am convinced a different atmosphere prevails today.

I cannot recollect the older players, when I first played against Lancashire, going into the opposition dressing-room to have a word before the day's play. If they passed in the corridor, they may have nodded and said 'Good morning', but that was the extent of the pleasantries. After that it was daggers drawn, and a 'no prisoners taken' attitude.

Nowadays the players are more socially minded, and a few of the senior caps have been on tour with some of the Lancashire team. This all helps to create a better relationship between the two sides.

I think, too, that people such as the Phil Sharpes, the Don Wilsons and John Hampshires are easier going, more relaxed than the Len Huttons, Bob Appleyards, Johnny Wardles of fifteen or so years ago. They still play their cricket hard, but without necessarily feeling that a smile or a murmured 'Well played' is an act of treason!

In my apprentice days, they used to reckon it would have been easier to travel south and play a Test match in front of a full house at Lord's than appear before a capacity crowd at Bramall Lane, Sheffield, or Old Trafford, Manchester. I could see the logic behind this theory. In a Test match the crowd is generally a cosmopolitan one, made up of people who want to see England win but not showing the passionate fervour of a Yorkshire or Lancashire crowd.

Those domestic battles up North always attracted huge gates—60 per cent urging on the home team, and 40 per cent clamouring for the away side. So whether you were playing on your own midden or your rivals', there were plenty of people rooting for you.

Mind you, although there is now a friendlier attitude between the two teams, a Yorkshireman still considers victory over Lancashire more important than any other success in the county championship.

Just in case he should question the importance of the fixture, there are always the retired players to put him straight. They look in the dressing-room and warn the team: 'Don't let this bloody lot do you.' Their grim expressions let you know that they want no truck with the 'enemy'. If you can't beat them, then get your head down and don't let them take you.

The 'Roses' games generally draw a lot of the older players. As the fixtures are staged over the Whitsun and August Bank holidays, they are free to attend and relive their own battles in the bars and tearooms. Sometimes, they tell me, there is more tension there than on the field!

The attitude of spectators to these Yorkshire *versus* Lancashire matches has certainly changed in recent years.

Not so long after I won a regular place in the Yorkshire side, I went into bat against Lancashire at Sheffield and we were around 50 for five. Brian Statham had slipped three or four out and Brian, with his tail up in those days, was a formidable foe. So Willie Watson and I dug in and added the best part of 200, but the early part of our stand was very slow. Yet the crowd appreciated the critical character of the situation confronting us. They saw it as a good battle and were prepared to sit through the struggle. Indeed, there was no barracking until the total had passed 150. After that they only complained if we didn't take our scoring chances when they came along. They were willing to give us a couple of hours to fight our way out of a tough position.

What happens today? I've gone to the wicket in the past few years and the barracking has started after I have faced only three or four balls.

I am old enough in the tooth to take it, but what about the lad going into his first 'Roses' clash? He needs encouragement. That type of crowd abuse can destroy him. It is all very well to talk about a player 'learning the hard way', but how can a youngster learn if his confidence has been shattered by ill-judged outbursts? Tensions on the field may have been tougher when I started, but at least the 'Roses' crowds were more knowledgeable and more understanding than they are today. I suppose it is all part of the modern cult to 'get on with it'. Even when you are 50 for five, they expect batsmen to be slogging the ball all over the ground.

Occasionally, you still get one of the old-time crowds. We did when we played at Old Trafford last August. That, you will recall, was Brian Statham's farewell appearance and after he had bowled us out for 61, Lancashire set Yorkshire a final target of scoring 253 to win in around five hours.

Lancashire had not beaten Yorkshire for eight years and when they took three wickets cheaply, it certainly looked as though the long period without success was finally to be ended. But Brian Close, with assistance from myself and Don Wilson, thwarted all the efforts of Statham, Kenny Higgs and Ken Shuttleworth.

That crowd, no doubt fascinated by the prospect of a Lancashire victory, understood their cricket. They only became exasperated when their own team let a chance or two slip.

Incidentally, Closey's not out innings of 77 was rated his most disciplined since he took that severe buffeting from Wes Hall and Charlie Griffith in the Lord's Test of 1963. He had decided to open the innings himself, and he took a lot of bruises on his thighs and shoulders before the game was drawn with Yorkshire 189 for five.

Afterwards he paid this tribute to Statham:

'Brian showed in this match what made him a great bowler. Right to the end he kept those qualities—pace, accuracy and control—that stamped him as one of the best of his, or any other, generation.

'In the past, Yorkshire have had many reasons to admire and respect him, and if his retirement comes as a great relief to the world's batsmen, it is a tremendous loss to the game of cricket.'

In recent seasons there has been a considerable fall-off in attendances at Yorkshire *versus* Lancashire matches. We used to have the gates closed on the Bank Holiday Monday with 30,000 inside, and the Saturday's play generally attracted 23,000 or more. Nowadays, if the weather is good, you will probably be lucky to draw 15,000.

The reasons for this decline are probably twofold: a general lessening of spectator interest at the gates and the fact that Lancashire have fielded a poor side for a number of years.

I think crowds are so partisan in Yorkshire and Lancashire that a Lancashire man cannot bear to go and sit in the crowd knowing, or almost certainly knowing, his side is going to receive a hiding. I am certain the same would apply to a Yorkshireman. If both teams are doing well, then the crowds will be there again. They have lost the habit of watching cricket in Lancashire because of this long period in the wilderness but, as I say, once they come good, you can expect the old 'ground full' notices to go up again.

I have talked about the changes in player-relationships and in crowd attitudes at these 'Roses' fixtures, but there is one other change which, to my mind, is more significant than the others. In recent years there has been a more determined effort by both counties to force victory, even if it has sometimes meant giving the opposition a chance of winning.

I know the Yorkshire players recognized that the outcome of the two 'Roses' fixtures could have an important bearing on the championship. It was all very well to stop the other side from winning, but a drawn game without points helped no one, except perhaps the consciences of some of the older players.

So, gradually there has developed a less defensive mentality in these games. The proportion of fixtures drawn may still be high, but at least there have been some desperately close finishes in the past few seasons. The teams have still been thinking of winning on the third day when some of their predecessors would have closed up shop and dismissed all thoughts of a bold gamble from their minds.

Few 'Roses' matches can have ended so dramatically as the 1960 meeting at Old Trafford, when Lancashire won off the very last ball. That, incidentally, was their first 'double' over Yorkshire since 1893.

Yorkshire did not seem to have an earthly chance when Lancashire began their final innings, wanting only 78 to win in a couple of hours. Yet Fred Trueman and Mel Ryan bowled with such tremendous fire and the whole team fielded as well as I have ever seen them, that when Tommy Greenhough was bowled by the second ball of Trueman's final over, five runs were still needed—and Lancashire had only two wickets left! In unbearable tension they snatched two singles and two leg-byes. Then Jackie Dyson—the same chap who won an F.A. Cup winner's medal with Manchester City in 1955–56—turned Fred's last ball to the on and Lancashire were home.

I say the Yorkshire fielding was magnificent, yet paradoxically, it was a lapse by the safest catcher of them all, Vic Wilson, which might have cost us victory. He dropped a dolly at mid-off at a vital stage in Lancashire's innings.

In physical and mental tension those two hours were harder than most full-days' play. But it was wonderful cricket. Lancashire had outplayed us for most of the match and thoroughly deserved to win. Those three days attracted 74,000 people—and they certainly had their money's worth.

I suppose of all the Lancashire players I have encountered, the hardest was Cyril Washbrook. 'Washie', with cap tilted, created authority whether he was strutting down the pavilion steps on his way to open an innings or hovering in the covers.

He brooked no interference as skipper and he seldom missed a trick in the field. You appreciated that when you were batting. We had people like Johnny Wardle, and Don Wilson, who could strike the spinners a long way but 'Washie' didn't give them the opportunity if he could help it. Immediately they arrived, he would call out: 'Brian, come and bowl this end', and Statham would come on, even if he had just bowled 30 overs. 'Washie' wouldn't give the tail-enders the chance of cutting loose against the slower men.

He was sometimes impatient, particularly with the younger players. I believe, too, he made a serious error of judgement when he dropped Roy Tattersall from the Lancashire side a few seasons ago. Roy was top of the English bowling averages at the time, with around 90 wickets, but 'Washie' decided he didn't spin the ball sufficiently. So out he went.

I doubt whether any man could play the game harder than Cyril. Since his retirement Lancashire have never seemed to field the same captain for very long at a time. The unsettled state of their leadership undoubtedly contributed to their decline, though I must say that when it came to 'Roses' games the atmosphere was less severe once Cyril had departed.

When people ask me if I regret the passing of the blood-and-guts type of cricket, I find it difficult to give a clear-cut answer. Obviously it is pleasanter playing today. On the other hand, a player must have experienced a great feeling of satisfaction in the kind of atmosphere prevailing before the war—and indeed, in the early years afterwards—when he hit a 'ton' or took six or seven wickets. I can imagine how delighted one must have felt batting for three or four hours while the fielding side cursed and cajoled you, and returning to the pavilion with 100 or so to your name. After all, if you could survive eleven scowling Lancastrians for the best part of a day, you must have learned a thing or two—and not just vocabulary!

Len Hutton, my schoolboy idol, was weaned on such occasions. He grew up in this unyielding atmosphere and it must have played a significant part in shaping his character. In my early days with Yorkshire, Len was a hard man to know. He kept very much to himself and the younger players never saw him from close of play until an hour before the next day's play. In those days the Yorkshire players did not stay in hotels booked by the county. Each player made his own arrangements. Consequently, the senior players tended to stay in the better class hotels while the rest of us congegated in cheaper places.

I never really understood Yorkshire's policy in leaving hotel bookings to the players. Team spirit was never good, but it might have been considerably better if we had all stayed in the same hotel. At least some of the capped players might have made more effort to help the youngsters if they had shared the same breakfast table.

We never met people like Len socially for a drink at night, and he never had much to say in the dressing-room. In fact, if he had not been so aloof, he could have achieved a great deal for the harmony of the side.

He was the one person who could really have sorted out

the petty jealousies and little cliques which bedevilled Yorkshire cricket when I was still learning my trade. Everyone
admired him as a great player. If he had asserted his
authority, he could have stopped the bickering. Unfortunately, he was content to sit back and let it all pass over his
head. It didn't affect him personally, so why should he
worry? That seemed to be his attitude. But it did affect the
younger players, who were so often the subject of biting
criticism from senior players. Quite a few of them either
never made the grade because their confidence was undermined or moved to other counties.

Len, of course, had great responsibilities as England's
leading batsman, and maybe he decided not to burden
himself with purely domestic problems, particularly as he
was not Yorkshire's captain.

Looking back at this distance in time, it seems incredible
that he was considered good enough to captain England, yet
apparently not good enough to skipper his native county.
I felt then that he should have been Yorkshire's captain and
so did many others inside the county. They say stubborn-
ness is a Yorkshire trait. Well, in pursuing the old amateur
tradition, the county committee certainly displayed it to
excess.

I believe that if Hutton had been given the captaincy he
would have gone on playing for Yorkshire for several more
seasons. He could have been a great source of inspiration
to the younger players. His knowledge of the game was considerable and he was so great a batsman technically that we
must have benefited. At that time, in the early 1950's, there
were five or six of us in our 'teens, among them Ken Taylor,
Doug Padgett and Brian Stott. Imagine the heady effect on
us of being led by *England's* captain! It smacks more of fiction,
yet it could have been fact for us if Yorkshire had shown
greater imagination.

Hutton played so many superb innings that it is difficult to single out any one knock of his. I know one which made a profound impression on me, and that was at Huddersfield. We were playing Worcestershire on a bad wicket. Reg Perks, always a lively type of bowler, used his height and strength to exploit this track and made the ball lift viciously. We were really struggling, but Len somehow played everything with time to spare.

Eventually, he completed 100 out of about 180. Almost immediately he took his bat away and just let them knock his hob down. It was as though the master was telling his pupils: That's how it should be done. Now you have a go!

On another occasion, Len played on a real dusty track at the Oval, with Jim Laker and Tony Lock in their prime. I think we managed only 138 all out and Len made 78. I don't think he played and missed more than one ball, yet everyone else was missing three or four times an over.

He made it look as though he was batting on a perfect wicket.

Len was the best bad-wicket player in the world, either against seamers or spin. He may have given his wicket away now and again, but not too often. He was too fond of making runs. Just because he happened to be dismissed a few times when he had reached his century doesn't mean he threw his innings away. Don't forget he was not a tremendously strong fellow physically. He was constantly under pressure both at county and at Test levels. People *expected* him to succeed. Was it any wonder, therefore, that sometimes his concentration lapsed once he had completed three figures?

Naturally, most players tend to relax once they have reached 100. The mental strain is on while the target is being attained. After that a batsman, provided he is not too tired physically, should be capable of many more runs, if his team requires them.

Of course, if a player has passed his century on a good

wicket and the score is around 300 for three, it is less important for him to stay. But if the rest of the batting is not showing much, he has a duty to remain as long as possible.

Some players need no second bidding. Geoffrey Boycott is an excellent example. He just wants to go on batting and batting. Even after six hours at the crease, he is determined to make the bowlers work for his wicket. He tends to treat his dismissal as an affront. Hours afterwards he will still be turning over the event in his mind or seeking to remedy the fault in his batting armoury at the nets. He could well be a latter-day Bradman—a coldly efficient run machine. The next few years will show whether he can sustain this present intensity of purpose.

A batsman in the runs can inspire colleagues, and also help new arrivals at the wicket by telling them how the pitch is playing. 'It's a very slow wicket, the slowest we've played on this season' or 'Just the odd one is turning a bit. It's not swinging much.' Such comments can be useful. Equally they can be misleading.

I recall one occasion when Jimmy Binks, the Yorkshire wicket-keeper, joined me at the wicket and asked if the ball was doing anything.

'Nothing is happening,' I replied. 'One hasn't turned since I've been here.' Almost immediately Jimmy got one which turned and down went his castle. When he walked out, he glared at me and muttered, 'Thank you very much, Raymond!' I was the first to buy him a drink that night—and he forgave me.

I found this exchange of advice much more prevalent with Yorkshire than with England. People tend to play more as individuals at Test level and, anyway, I imagine they think to themselves: This player wouldn't have been picked for England if he couldn't read what's going on out in the middle.

24

Too many changes

'Bewitched, bothered and bewildered' runs the title of a well-known song. It could be applied equally to cricket's followers during the past twenty years or so.

No game surely has suffered such a mass of changes to its laws and regulations in such a brief period of its history.

We have had experiments on taking the new ball, limitation of the leg-side field, declarations, pitch covering, the follow-on.

We have been caught up in long-drawn-out arguments on throwing, polishing the ball, the bowler's drag.

We have scratched our heads in puzzlement at the incredible number of permutations drawn up for obtaining County Championship points.

No wonder that people are asking us: Why can't they leave the game alone? They are ruining it with all this tinkering about with the rules.

The ordinary follower goes to cricket because he wants to be entertained. In recent years he must often have gone home at the end of a day's play wondering whether the principal participants—committees, groundsmen, umpires, captains and players—were too involved in fulfilling the requirements of the regulations to worry about box-office appeal.

I think part of the trouble originally stemmed from a misconception—the idea that county cricket could win back the crowds in midweek.

The Advisory County Cricket Committee and all the special committees and research teams now know that only a comparative few have the time to spare to watch the game on the Tuesday, Wednesday, Thursday and Friday.

So the time could be approaching when we may have to consider one four-day match each week, covering, say, Friday, Saturday, Sunday and Monday, and one full-day or half-day knock-out or league game.

For years people have been saying that most of the so-called ills of the game would disappear if we had really good wickets on which to play our matches.

I disagree. I think the wickets can be too good for three-day cricket. They should be good enough for a competent team to win in that time instead of having to introduce freak declarations to make a definite result possible.

If on good English wickets county teams cannot obtain definite results without recourse to these contrived finishes, we should go for four-day championship fixtures. It works very well in Australia.

I think all the worst cricket that Yorkshire played over the last two years occurred on very good wickets. Yorkshire knew that there was virtually no chance of bowling out the other side, who would bat a day and half and all one could hope for was declarations. When a side is determined to make a big first innings total on a really good strip and bat, say, to lunchtime on the second day, the cricket can become awfully dreary.

Let me stress here that I am not against three-day cricket played on wickets which give a fair chance to both batsmen *and* bowlers.

If a change in the match structure does become necessary, I hope we shall not allow the county game to develop into one-day fixtures. I know that they appeal to many folk who like to see a finish, but they do bring out many of the worst aspects of cricket.

The Gillette Cup and the one-day league encourage selection committees to bank on medium-pace bowlers, bowling to defensive fields. That was not the way I was brought up to play the game, nor, I suspect, were many other cricketers.

In Yorkshire we were always brought up to try to bowl the batsman out. Not to bowl wide of the stumps, but to bowl straight.

My fear is that if a lot of this one-day cricket is permitted, it won't be long—a few years—before there will be no young spinners coming into the game. After all, what will be the incentive for them to enter when the emphasis is on medium pace?

I hope my fears are misplaced. It would be a sorry day for the game if spinners no longer had a part to play in it. We have already seen the decline and fall of the leg-spin breed— and all the experts now bewail their absence.

I know I have a vested interest, but I believe there can be few more compelling sights in cricket than a battle of wits between a good-class spinner and a good-class batsman.

The introduction of one four-day match each week would also give the players a little more spare time and cut down the costs of travelling. I believe you can lose a little bit of enthusiasm by playing six days a week non-stop throughout the season.

Personally, the present form of the county game does not have that effect on me. I look forward to every game. The only thing I find is that by the middle of August, when I have been bowling a lot of overs, I begin to feel a shade tired. But that shouldn't be confused with lack of enthusiasm. I repeat, I look forward to every game.

The bonus points which were introduced last summer to encourage more positive play worked out reasonably well. My only reservation concerns the effect of its workings on the younger batsman, the chap who has just been given his chance in the first-class game.

He may have to throw his wicket away simply in order that his side can collect an extra bonus point. It can happen more especially with teams at the top of the county table.

Now I cannot believe that it is beneficial, in the long term, for young players to be committed in this way. Imagine yourself as a raw recruit to the county side, walking in to face Brian Statham and knowing that you are expected to have a go at getting 20 runs off the next three overs. You lash out hopefully and are 'castled'. All right, you have thrown away your wicket trying to carry out orders, but what will these low scores do for your morale? And will the county committee, when they review your performances and averages at the end of the summer, say to themselves: 'So-and-so was out cheaply a number of times but, ah! of course, we got him chasing bonus points.'

When I consider the various law changes while I have been playing, I cannot help thinking that the off-spin bowler has been affected more than any other bowler.

A number of these law revisions were designed to stop the medium-pace bowlers bowling to leg-side fields. In fact, they penalized the off-spinners, particularly on turning wickets.

If you have any old photographs of legside fields set by off-break bowlers, they are worth re-examining. In the days before the restrictions were imposed, both my short legs would always be behind square, mainly because we used to bowl middle stump or even middle to leg.

As we were then permitted to have as many fielders as we wanted on the leg side and where we wanted them, we could afford to put two short legs behind the wicket and a man deep square, behind deep square, and also behind deep wicket, if needed.

These placings made it harder for the batsman to score because we were bowling at his legs all the time. But then the new rule was framed which stipulated that you could only have five fielders on the legside, two behind square.

Immediately the off-spinner had to move his line across,

probably six inches, and bowl off stump or just outside. This was because if he continued bowling on the old line, the batsman could pick it up and hit it over square leg where there was only one man back to cover the whole leg side.

I have found it fascinating looking at more recent photographs of my field placings to see how the short legs have become so much squarer. We won more scope when the law-makers decided that you could have as many fielders as you liked on the legside, provided only two were behind.

In discussions I have had with the administrators, they have agreed that the changed laws have certainly penalized the off-spinner, though not by intention. They wanted to stop such instances as the occasion when Trevor Bailey bowled down the legside in a Test match against the Australians; the time, in the early 1950's when the West Indies, in danger of defeat by Yorkshire, bowled outside the leg stump with eight fielders posted on the legside.

However, as off-spinners still seem to be surviving and taking a fair share of wickets, I suppose we mustn't complain too strongly!

In looking back on my career, I do not have to search far for my most moving experience. It came when I bowled for the last time for Yorkshire in the Scarborough Festival last summer. The band played 'For He's a Jolly Good Fellow', 'Goodbyee' and 'Ilkley Moor' and the crowd applauded. Believe me, there was a lump in my throat.

If I were offered my time again, I would have no hesitation in choosing the same career. I believe most county players would take a similar decision.

Cricket offers a constant challenge to your skills. It also offers you the opportunity of meeting distinguished names in other walks of life. If you are fortunate, too, you will visit many parts of the world with M.C.C. teams.

Above all, there is the friendship which exists between players of the various seventeen first-class county clubs. It is certainly something which you will find in few other major sports. I have always thought it a pity that professional footballers do not socialize more at inter-club level. The goodwill of such occasions can rub off on the field and that, surely, can only be for the benefit of the sport as a whole.

Whatever shape the county championships takes in the years ahead, I am confident the game itself, from village green to Test arena, will go on providing pleasure for millions. May you be among them.

APPENDIX

Ray Illingworth

Career Statistics compiled by Bill Frindall

ALL FIRST-CLASS MATCHES

BATTING AND FIELDING SUMMARY

Season	M.	I.	N.O.	Runs	H.S.	Avge.	100s	50s	Catches
1951	1	1	0	56	56	56·00	–	1	–
1952	6	6	2	152	48	38·00	–	–	2
1953	34	40	11	823	146*	28·37	1	2	11
1954	24	33	5	426	59	15·21	–	2	14
1955	28	36	6	1,040	138	34·66	2	5	24
1956	34	46	8	755	78	19·86	–	4	12
1957	33	52	9	1,213	97	28·20	–	8	17
1958	32	46	9	643	81*	17·37	–	2	12
1959	33	50	13	1,726	162	46·64	5	5	30
1959–60	12	16	2	353	100	25·31	1	2	3
1960	33	49	10	1,006	86	25·79	–	4	25
1960–61	4	6	2	83	31	20·75	–	–	3
1961	34	51	4	1,153	75	24·53	–	8	25
1962	36	56	9	1,612	127	34·29	3	8	28
1962–63	12	16	3	329	65*	25·30	–	2	10
1963	22	31	5	676	107*	26·00	1	–	15
1964	33	44	9	1,301	135	37·17	2	7	17
1965	32	47	8	916	90	23·48	–	3	25
1966	27	39	8	673	98	21·70	–	2	22
1967	27	36	9	759	68*	28·11	–	4	8
1968	31	37	9	819	100*	29·25	1	3	16
	528	738	141	16,514	162	27·66	16	72	319

BOWLING SUMMARY

Season	Balls	M.	Runs	Wkts.	Avge.	5 Wkts. Inns.	10 Wkts. Mtch.
1951	–	–	–	–	–	–	–
1952	606	26	227	7	32·42	–	–
1953	4,878	240	2,023	75	26·97	2	–
1954	1,854	93	683	25	27·32	1	1
1955	3,534	196	1,358	48	28·29	–	–
1956	3,726	206	1,348	103	13·08	5	1
1957	4,998	287	1,951	106	18·40	7	1
1958	4,304	223	1,621	92	17·61	7	–
1959	6,247	340	2,361	110	21·46	3	–
1959–60	2,190	107	781	11	71·00	–	–

Season	Balls	M.	Runs	Wkts.	Avge.	5 Wkts. Inns.	10 Wkts. Mtch
1960	5,955	422	1,914	109	17·55	7	1
1960–61	516	23	240	5	48·00	–	–
1961	6,591	434	2,292	128	17·90	9	1
1962	6,488	426	2,276	117	19·45	8	–
1962–63	1,793	55	709	17	41·70	–	–
1963	2,902	170	1,078	60	17·96	4	–
1964	6,074	374	2,131	122	17·46	7	1
1965	5,124	360	1,630	98	16·63	6	–
1966	4,981	316	1,680	100	16·80	8	1
1967	5,289	365	1,613	101	15·97	6	2
1968	5,744	360	1,882	131	14·36	7	2
	83,794	5,023	29,798	1,565	19·04	87	11

Balls per wicket: 53·5
Runs per 100 balls: 35·6

OVERSEAS TOURS

1959–60   M.C.C. in the West Indies
1960–61   Cavaliers in South Africa and Rhodesia
1962–63   M.C.C. in Australia and New Zealand

HUNDREDS (16)

For *Yorkshire* (14)

v. Essex: 146* at Hull, 1953
116   at Southend, 1955
150   at Colchester, 1959

v. Hampshire: 115 at Bournemouth, 1962
v. Kent: 135 at Dover, 1964
v. Leicestershire: 100* at Sheffield, 1968
v. Surrey: 127 at The Oval, 1962
v. Sussex: 122 at Hove, 1959
v. Warwickshire: 107 at Sheffield, 1962
107* at Birmingham, 1963
v. M.C.C.: 138 at Scarborough, 1955
105* at Scarborough, 1959
103 at Scarborough, 1964
v. Indians: 162 at Sheffield, 1959

* Not out.

For *M.C.C.* (1)
v. Berbice: 100 at Blairmont, Berbice, 1959–60
For *Players* (1)
v. Gentleman: 100 at Lord's, 1959

BEST BOWLING PERFORMANCES

(*a*) *Seven or more wickets in an innings* (19)
For *Yorkshire* (18)
v. Essex: 7—49 at Middlesbrough, 1958
v. Glamorgan: 8—70⎫ at Swansea, 1960
                  7—53⎭
v. Gloucestershire: 7—58⎫ at Harrogate, 1967
                       7— 6⎭
v. Hampshire: 7–22 at Bournemouth, 1953
                7—39 at Bournemouth, 1961
v. Kent: 7—49⎫ at Dover, 1964
            7—52⎭
v. Lancashire: 8—50 at Manchester, 1961
v. Northamptonshire: 7—40 at Northampton, 1962
v. Nottinghamshire: 7—89 at Scarborough, 1964
v. Surrey: 8—69 at The Oval, 1954
             7—62 at The Oval, 1964
v. Warwickshire: 7—54 at Middlesbrough, 1961
v. Worcestershire: 9—42 at Worcester, 1957
                     (His best innings analysis.)
                     8—20 at Leeds, 1965
v. M.C.C.: 7—73 at Scarborough, 1968
For *An England XI* (1)
v. Young England: 7—51 at Scarborough, 1963

(*b*) *Ten or more wickets in a match* (11)
For *Yorkshire* (11)
v. Glamorgan: 15—123 at Swansea, 1960
v. Gloucestershire: 14—64 at Harrogate, 1967

  v. Hampshire: 12—102 at Bournemouth, 1961
  v. Kent: 14—101 at Dover, 1964
  v. Leicestershire: 11—126 at Leicester, 1966
                       11—79 at Leicester, 1967
  v. Surrey: 10—110 at The Oval, 1954
  v. Warwickshire: 10—71 at Middlesbrough, 1968
  v. Worcestershire: 10—62 at Bradford, 1956
                       12—91 at Worcester, 1957
                       10—79 at Sheffield, 1968

ALL-ROUND ACHIEVEMENTS

Illingworth has done the 'Double', scoring 1,000 runs and taking 100 wickets, on six occasions. This feat has been surpassed by only two other Yorkshire players: Wilfred Rhodes (16) and George Hirst (14).

Season	Runs	Avge.	Wkts	Avge.
1957	1,213	28·20	106	18·40
1959	1,726	46·64	110	21·46
1960	1,006	25·79	109	17·55
1961	1,153	24·53	128	17·90
1962	1,612	34·29	117	19·45
1964	1,301	37·17	122	17·46

With 16,514 runs and 1,565 wickets, Illingworth is only the third Yorkshire player—and the eighteenth in all first-class cricket—to exceed 15,000 runs and 1,500 wickets in his career.

Against Kent at Dover, in 1964, Illingworth scored a century and took fourteen wickets in the match: 135 and 7—49 and 7—52. There have been only six other post-war instances of this particular match double in England. By coincidence, the next—and most recent—instance was also against Kent at Dover; by Garfield Sobers in 1968.

PLAYERS *v.* GENTLEMEN AT LORD'S

Illingworth was only once selected for the Players in this historic series of annual matches which ended with the abolition of amateur status in English cricket after the 1962 season. However, this single appearance in 1959 was sufficient for him to enter his name in the record books by scoring 100 and sharing in a seventh-wicket partnership of 184 with Brian Close. This is the highest partnership for that wicket by the Players against the Gentlemen in the entire series of matches dating back to 1806.

IN TEST CRICKET

BATTING AND FIELDING

Season	Against	M.	I.	N.O.	Runs	H.S.	Avge.	100s	50s	Catches
1958	New Zealand	1	1	1	3	3*	–	–	–	–
1959	India	2	3	1	118	50	59·00	–	1	5
1959–60	West Indies	5	8	1	92	41*	13·14	–	–	1
1960	South Africa	4	6	2	81	37	20·25	–	–	1
1961	Australia	2	3	–	28	15	9·33	–	–	5
1962	Pakistan	1	1	1	2	2*	–	–	–	–
1962–63	Australia	2	3	–	57	27	19·00	–	–	–
1962–63	New Zealand	3	3	–	68	46	22·66	–	–	4
1965	New Zealand	1	–	–	–	–	–	–	–	–
1966	West Indies	2	3	–	7	4	2·33	–	–	2
1967	India	3	4	1	28	12*	9·33	–	–	2
1967	Pakistan	1	2	–	13	9	6·50	–	–	–
1968	Australia	3	4	–	51	27	12·75	–	–	1
		30	41	7	548	50	16·11	–	1	21

Summary

Against	M.	I.	N.O.	Runs	H.S.	Avge.
Australia	7	10	–	136	27	13·60
South Africa	4	6	2	81	37	20·25
West Indies	7	11	1	99	41*	9·90
New Zealand	5	4	1	71	46	23·66
India	5	7	2	146	50	29·20
Pakistan	2	3	1	15	9	7·50
	30	41	7	548	50	16·11

	M.	I.	N.O.	Runs	H.S.	Avge.
In England	20	27	6	331	50	15·76
Overseas	10	14	1	217	46	16·69

* Not out

BOWLING

Season	Against	Balls	M.	Runs	Wkts.	Avge.
1958	New Zealand	270	18	59	3	19·66
1959	India	510	33	124	4	31·00
1959–60	West Indies	1,176	61	383	4	95·75
1960	South Africa	462	32	146	6	24·33
1961	Australia	333	17	126	3	42·00
1962	Pakistan	204	14	81	1	81·00
1962–63	Australia	320	9	131	1	131·00
1962–63	New Zealand	270	20	73	5	14·60
1965	New Zealand	210	14	70	4	17·50
1966	West Indies	378	24	165	4	41·25
1967	India	927	68	266	20	13·30
1967	Pakistan	276	25	58	3	19·33
1968	Australia	1,100	82	291	13	22·38
		6,436	417	1,973	71	27·78

Balls per wicket: 90·6
Runs per 100 balls: 30·7

Summary

Against	Balls	M.	Runs	Wkts.	Avge.
Australia	1,753	108	548	17	32·23
South Africa	462	32	146	6	24·33
West Indies	1,554	85	548	8	68·50
New Zealand	750	52	202	12	16·83
India	1,437	101	390	24	16·25
Pakistan	480	39	139	4	34·75
	6,436	417	1,973	71	27·78

	Balls	M.	Runs	Wkts.	Avge.
In England	4,670	327	1,386	61	22·72
Overseas	1,766	90	587	10	58·70

Five wickets in an innings (2):

6—29 v. India at Lord's, 1967
6—87 v. Australia at Leeds, 1968

MEMORABILIA

Playing for M.C.C. against Berbice at Blairmont, British Guiana, on the 1959–60 tour, Illingworth (100) was one of seven M.C.C. batsmen (the first seven in the order) who scored fifty or more. This equalled the world record set by the 1938 Australians against Oxford University.

Illingworth took 14 wickets after lunch on the second day of Yorkshire's vital match against Gloucestershire at Harrogate in September, 1967. His figures of 23—8—58—7 and 13—9—6—7 gave Yorkshire an innings victory in two days and the championship. Illingworth took his first wicket at 2.24 p.m. and his last at 6.45 p.m.—14 wickets in 224 minutes of actual playing time or a wicket every 16 minutes. He was twice on a hat-trick.

On his final appearance for Yorkshire in 1968, Illingworth took 7—73 against M.C.C. at Scarborough. This took his aggregate for the season to 131—a personal record and the highest number of wickets by any bowler in 1968.